Whose Values?

"Since 1888, we have been molding boys into splendid, clean-thinking young men."

— the Headmaster, Pencey Prep,
Agerstown, Pennsylvania.
From J.D. Salinger, *The Catcher in the Rye*

Whose Values?
Reflections of a New England Prep School Teacher

A Study of Values and the American Independent School

Barbara Bernache-Baker

Phi Delta Kappa Educational Foundation
Bloomington, Indiana, U.S.A.

Cover design by
Victoria Voelker

Phi Delta Kappa Educational Foundation
408 North Union Street
Post Office Box 789
Bloomington, Indiana 47402-0789
U.S.A.

Library of Congress Catalog Card Number 00-111021
ISBN 0-87367-831-1

To all of my students and faculty
colleagues, past and present,
who have taught me so very much.

FOREWORD

Two of the author's former students, one from her first decade of teaching and one from the last, provide this Foreword.

It was my great good luck to have been Barbara Bernache-Baker's student at Mount Hermon School in 1957, and I still am learning from her more than 40 years later. In my case, her class instilled more than an avid love of biology and a lifelong affinity with biologists — I married one and helped raise an arachnologist daughter and an ornithologist son, an example, I suppose, of the ripple effect great teachers can have. Mrs. Baker (as we called her then) was expecting her first child when I was in her class, and so the wonders of human reproduction bloomed before our eyes (and ears as well, as we were allowed to listen to the fetal heartbeat through a stethoscope placed on her rapidly swelling abdomen). As for introducing us young lads to sex back in those bygone days before the so-called revolution, Barbara Bernache-Baker was most certainly always quite proper. Yet she possessed such a fresh spirit and joyful commitment to scientific honesty, her teaching spoke to us in a profound, life-affecting way.

Now, with this long–needed book, others also will have a chance to learn from Barbara Bernache-Baker. Her meticulous research and provocative reflections combine here to offer fresh perspectives into the heart of what a values-centered education is — or, at least, should be — about. She brings her scientific background to bear on many levels of the complex boarding school environment. She notes the often significant differences existing between what the schools in her study say and what they actually do. Here, as in her teaching, Barbara Bernache-Baker is still making meaningful connections. As she makes quite clear, her book is not meant to be the last word on the complex subject of sexuality and values, but rather to encourage the sort of dialogue every family, school, and community should be having. Some will embrace the topics discussed with more enthusiasm than others. Those afraid of the subject or uncomfortable with her findings may be most in need of this book and the honest exploration it encourages. Others may find it merely useful, but all will find it illuminating. Most important, Barbara goes beyond her statistically based findings to become a true healer, encouraging here the long-term good will of the independent school community.

This book will be especially therapeutic for those still suffering the effects of distortions encountered as boarding school students. In recent years, as class secretary for an alumni magazine, I have been surprised at how many classmate communications have expressed ambivalence about their old school concerning just such issues that Barbara sheds light on here. Decade after decade, these fellows are still troubled by the gap between the reality of the experience of self and the "role-model" images impressed on them during their boarding school years. Indeed, a retired Bible teacher of the old school even expressed remorse to me shortly before his death over not having challenged the provincialisms prevalent at the school years before, including some of the very issues that Barbara has had the courage and insight to discuss.

For boarding schools to remain in the forefront of our education efforts, they must offer a living example of core values fully attuned to a rapidly changing world. They can no longer be comfortable repositories for self-delusion and hypocrisy, offering only a "don't look, don't see, don't tell" split-brain approach to emotionally charged topics of the day. To justify their existence today, all schools, public and private, must express a commitment to a love of learning, a genuine appreciation for diversity (both natural and intellectual), and a truly wholesome integrity. These just happen to be the values that Barbara Bernache-Baker has so wonderfully modeled in her teaching, life, and now in this book. Readers will find no ulterior motives here — only an honest effort to help the prep school community she so obviously loves. That's what I call a great teacher. I hope the readers of this book will experience at least some of the intellectual excitement I've experienced since entering her classroom over 40 years ago.

Richard Bodner

Writer-poet Bodner graduated from Mount Hermon School (now the co-educational Northfield Mount Hermon School) in the class of 1960 and attended Harvard University. He currently resides in Las Vegas, New Mexico.

* * *

Barbara Bernache-Baker has been a source of inspiration throughout my adult life. I first encountered her as my biology teacher at the Loomis Chaffee School in 1981, where she became my academic advisor and mentor for the next three years. Her style of teaching inspired insightful thinking about nature, the environment, and science. Her enthusiasm extended to all of her classes and laboratories. She always emphasized the mode of observation and hypothesis formulation that lies at the heart of the scientific process. Dr. Bernache-Baker has practiced these methods herself with great success and here provides her readers with a highly provocative look at the vitally important areas of sexuality and value formulation within independent schools.

Maria Gluch, M.D.

Dr. Gluch graduated from the Loomis Chaffee School in 1985 and attended Connecticut College and the University of Connecticut Medical School. She completed her residency in obstetrics and gynecology at the University of Virginia Medical School and currently holds a position as attending physician and clinical instructor at the Harvard University Medical School. Gluch currently is involved with the Jewish Community Relations Council of Greater Boston and the Beth Israel Deaconess Department of Obstetric and Gynecology, training physicians in primary and preventive gynecological and pediatric care in Dnepropetrovsk, Ukraine, and providing free care for thousands of Ukrainian women and children.

PREFACE

In late August 1954 my husband entered the long campus driveway of the Mount Hermon School for Boys in Massachusetts to interview for a teaching job. To this day he can recall the thrill he felt as he viewed the beauty of the campus and the surrounding Pioneer Valley country. This, plus the warm and captivating personality of the headmaster who interviewed him, the late Howard L. Rubendall, led him into a state of mind such that he accepted the job for an eighth of what he was making in industry. Small matter that he was replacing a person who had resigned only days before classes were to begin and thus was in a salary bargaining position of considerable strength — the thought never crossed his mind. The love he felt for the school was instant and, like one's first crush, remains with him still.

I understand his feelings. I had experienced them only two years before when I left research at Harvard University and the Woods Hole Oceanographic Institute to join the faculty of Cushing Academy in the lovely village of Ashburnham, Massachusetts. Since then, I have taught at three other New England college preparatory schools; but Cushing will always hold a special place in my heart. At Cushing, as a single woman faculty member, I lived in a female student dormitory and ate all of my meals with the students and faculty in the main dining hall. I then experienced prep school life as a married faculty member living in a dormitory at Mount Hermon School and, still later, with my growing family in a school-owned house just off the Mount Hermon campus. My final years of prep school teaching were spent as a day faculty member at the Loomis Chaffee School in Windsor, Connecticut. Thus by fortuitous circumstance I have had an opportunity to view prep school life from several very different perspectives. It is from these perspectives that I write.

Over the past several years, much interest has developed in "preppies," those secondary school students who attend privately owned and funded college preparatory schools, or "prep schools."

Cartoonist Garry Trudeau, in his syndicated cartoon strip "Doonesbury," once devoted several days to this uniquely perceived adolescent. The success of such commercial ventures as preppie clothing and hairstyles and sufficient sales of *The Official Preppie Handbook* (1980) to keep it a best seller for several weeks reflect this interest. On the more serious side, many magazine articles about college preparatory schools and guidelines designed to help in selecting them, written primarily for the parents of prospective students, are popular items in bookstores and libraries. Equally significant, biographies of such eminent prep school graduates as presidents Franklin Delano Roosevelt (Groton) and John F. Kennedy (then Choate, now the coeducational Choate–Rosemary Hall) mention the cradling of their developing political minds within the privileged walls of their respective institutions.* While I was carrying out the research that led to this book, some noteworthy prep school graduates included the President of the United States, George Bush (Phillips Academy, Andover) and both United States senators from my home state of Connecticut, Christopher Dodd (Georgetown Preparatory School) and Lowell Weicker (Lawrenceville).** Weicker later served as governor of Connecticut. Surveys of the secondary schools attended by persons either elected or appointed to positions of national and even international political power — for example, Ronald Reagan's secretary of state George Schultz (Loomis Chaffee) and Jordan's Queen Noor (Concord Academy) — show an influence wielded by prep school graduates that is dispropor-

---

*In 1946, speaking at his school's 50th anniversary dinner, 29-year-old Congressman John F. Kennedy chided Choate and other prep schools for not making a contribution to the field of politics. Considering the role that Franklin Delano Roosevelt had played in the Kennedy family's political development (JFK's father, Joseph Kennedy, was FDR's ambassador to England), the statement is an unusual one. Ironically, in 1960, Kennedy would be locked in a brief struggle with another Choate graduate, Adlai Stevenson, Class of 1918, for the Democratic party's nomination to be its candidate for the presidency.
**While I was checking the proofs for this book, it was announced that former President Bush's son, George W., also a Phillips Andover graduate, is to be the next president, narrowly defeating Vice President Al Gore, a graduate of St. Albans School.

tionate to any figure that might be predicted by chance. Nor is this a recent phenomenon. More than a quarter of Phillips Exeter Academy graduates between 1920 and 1929 held elected or appointed public offices, and at Groton the record was even more impressive. For this reason alone, it is well worth paying attention to the role such schools play in the formation of their students' ethical and sociopolitical viewpoints.

The idea for this book arose from research carried out for my Ph.D. dissertation. My study was designed to see if there are significant differences in value-based attitudes and behaviors between prep school students and their closest public school counterparts, that is, public school graduates who are, like almost all prep school students, college bound.

There are several reasons for conducting such a study. First, of course, is that new knowledge has value for its own sake, exclusive of any utilitarian purpose. In addition, there currently is a great deal of political pressure — emanating mostly, but not entirely, from the so-called Religious Right — to allow the use of tax dollars to support nonpublic, mostly religious schools on the ground that such schools instill good values in their students.

Beyond that, as a college preparatory school teacher, it was of considerable interest to me to determine if the perceived differences between prep school students and non-prep school adolescents are, in fact, genuine. Certainly many people believe they are. Each morning on my drive to teach my classes at Loomis Chaffee, graffiti on a Hartford public park wall instructed me to "kill preppies." Clearly, the graffiti author viewed the students I was teaching as a distinctly different (and expendable) species. From my own research, it was evident that many of the prep school students in my sample also viewed themselves that way. Commenting on this self-image, a 1950s prep school graduate wrote:

> We ought to be thinking about the relationship between ourselves and those educated in the public school system. The air of superiority hanging over those educated in independent schools is all too evident. (*The Kent News*, 23 April 1988)

Most significant, however, is that prep schools also portray themselves as institutions possessing special qualities. Seemingly foremost among these qualities is the inculcation of ethical or moral values. In their promotional literature, college preparatory schools often imply that they provide an environment in which stronger and more pervasive value systems develop than is possible elsewhere ("values to guide them throughout their lives" with an emphasis on "moral and social responsibility" is the way one school puts it in its promotional literature), the "elsewhere" presumably being the public schools. John Sedgwick, a 1970s Groton graduate, quotes headmaster William Polk:

> I always get faintly nervous when people ask me the number of Groton graduates in the State Department, because that is not what the school's about. This school is about character. It's a word that went out of favor in the 1960s. That's too bad. It's a good word. It means living life with integrity, caring about those around them. (Sedgwick 1988)

Not only do prep schools lay claim to a moral higher ground, they often suggest reasons for why they occupy it. David Black, headmaster of Salem Academy in Winston-Salem, North Carolina, puts it quite succinctly:

> Independent high schools have one thing that public schools often don't. A private school can present a moral ethos. It can articulate certain principles and when students sign a pledge they promise to follow those principles. So at the very beginning you start with shared experiences. (quoted in "Of Arts and Sciences" 1994)

A final reason for this study is that it does more than reveal the attitudes and behavior of the sample populations. I realized that, by combining my research results with my own "insider view" of college preparatory schools, I might help illuminate some possible causes for the problems that often beset such schools. But such a combination made it difficult to find a publisher. One scholarly press considered placing the book in a series of monographs dealing with various aspects of sociological research. (I could not think of a better way to ensure that the book would not reach its intended audience.) At the other extreme, a trade book agent wanted the book, but insisted that I rewrite it so as to emphasize the "juicier" results of my research.

Thus the enthusiastic reception of my manuscript by Donovan R. Walling, the director of publications and research for Phi Delta Kappa International, was most welcome — especially in light of the PDK's long history of supporting both public and private education at all levels. It was a nice conclusion to our efforts to locate a highly reputable publisher with a genuine interest in education as well as one willing to take a chance on my book pretty much in the same format that I had written it.

Some of my research results will be reported where appropriate throughout this work. For those who may find the methods, statistical analyses, and tabular data rather tedious, a written summary is provided in an appendix, along with references to the research of others that is pertinent to my work. This information is included for researchers who might wish to carry out a similar investigation.

My promise of confidentiality to the staff, students, administrators, and faculty that I sampled or interviewed while carrying out my research preclude any personal identifications, with or without their school affiliations. However, I found myself going back and forth on whether to identify the precise college preparatory school at which a particular incident occurred. The final decision not to do so was based primarily on my observation of a tendency on the part of school administrations to relax when some other school is involved. Theodore Sizer made the same decision for precisely that reason in his book *Horace's Compromise: The Dilemma of the American High School.* Sizer, now chair of the Coalition of Essential Schools at Brown University and a former headmaster of Phillips Academy, Andover, manages to relate real incidents he observed at the schools included in his study in a manner that conveys devastating criticism in positive and constructive ways. He writes in his preface:

> The characters here portrayed are real people, and the places described are all actual places. With but a few, most-

ly personal exceptions, however, I have masked true identities. It has been my experience that educators tend to ignore something not exactly on their own turf. "Oh that's Lincoln High School," they say; "it can't apply to us." The points I am trying to make do in fact extend beyond any one high school, and I wish no reader to think otherwise. (1984, pp. 7-8)

This same reasoning applies to my sampled prep schools: They, too, share remarkably similar atmospheres and philosophies; and incidents described at one school could just as easily have happened at another. Indeed, they usually have. Thus I have elected to identify individual schools only when dealing with material clearly of a non-confidential nature. In addition, when a school conveys in its magazines, promotional literature, or non-confidential memos a policy or education philosophy many find disturbing or even appalling, I see no reason to protect that school by concealing its identity.

I wish to thank Cushing Academy, located in Ashburnham, Massachusetts, for first introducing me to the joys of prep school teaching. The Mount Hermon School for Boys and Northfield School for Girls (now the coeducational Northfield Mount Hermon) in Northfield, Massachusetts, enabled me to continue and to enhance this experience.

Heartfelt thanks also must go to the late Frederick G. Torrey, a very fine person I first knew as a faculty colleague at Mount Hermon, for bringing me away from laboratory research in the biology department at Wesleyan University and back into teaching at the Loomis Chaffee School in Windsor, Connecticut, where he had moved to become headmaster.

Special thanks are particularly appropriate for Torrey's replacement, John R. Ratté, for his support and that of Loomis Chaffee in helping me with this task. It speaks well for the school that it did so, for I often spoke openly and critically of some of its policies during the 15 years I was a faculty member there. Dr. Ratté once wrote me: "Don't try to anticipate what people will think of your book. If you tell the truth, you will get hit on the head, says an ancient Jewish proverb — there's no avoiding it. But only truth-telling will help us to grow." I have tried to follow this very wise advice.

So many persons become involved in a project of this sort that it becomes impossible to thank them all. Foremost among these, of course, are the students and faculty who composed the sample populations, many of whom expressed such enthusiastic interest in what I was doing that it could not help but be catching. Many friends, including school heads, faculty, and students, past and present, read all or portions of the manuscript and made many helpful criticisms and suggestions. To all of these, especially those who provided additional insights during personal interviews, I give heartfelt thanks. Similarly, I am indebted to my dissertation committee, Lewis Durham, the late Loretta Haroian, the late Wardell Pomeroy, and Robert Sorensen, for their helpful advice and encouragement. Sincere thanks go also to Janet Morgan and George Zepco of the Wesleyan University Computer Center for their assistance in introducing me to the proper programs and allowing frequent access to their personal expertise; David "Ness" Cohen, who at times worked with me at the computer terminal, literally through the night, explaining patiently the various access codes; Karl Scheibe, professor of psychology and statistics, Wesleyan University; and Margaret Ely, professor of psychology, New York University, for their helpful suggestions concerning research design and appropriate statistical analysis; Jill Morawski, then associate professor of psychology, Wesleyan University, for her assurance that my research techniques were in keeping with ethical guidelines for social science research; Aaron Hass, Department of Psychiatry, University of California at Los Angeles School of Medicine, for sharing his experiences and ideas from his own research concerning the obtaining of population samples; Dale Clayton, of the Loomis Chaffee School Brush Library, for his aid in questionnaire design and preparation; the Reverend Peter Vorkink, teacher and former chair of the religion department at Phillips Exeter Academy, for his helpful comments on Chapter 4, Religion and Values; Teresa L. Tate (née Lowe), former prep school employee and research assistant extraordinaire, whose many trips to the library and patient word-processor typing and retyping of all of this is most deeply appreciated; and other independent school faculty and administrators, too numerous to list, who were kind enough to read all or part of my manuscript and make many valuable suggestions. I want to thank my editor at Phi Delta Kappa, David Ruetschlin, for helping me understand the book production process, as well as his patience in dealing with my objections to some of his changes. I know that *Whose Values?* is a far better book because of his efforts. Finally, I must thank Jeffrey J.W. Baker, my best friend and life partner for more than 45 years. As a prep school graduate (Christchurch School, Urbanna, Virginia) and a former prep school teacher before becoming a college professor, his gift for creating an appropriate analogy or finding the perfect passage to further illuminate a point, as well as his consummate skill as an editor, played a major role in the organization and occasional rewriting of my scribbled or verbally expressed thoughts into what I trust will be a readable book.

Let me close this preface by putting this work into its proper perspective. It deals both with research carried out on a sampling of the New England area college preparatory school world as it existed in the early 1980s and the subjective impressions of the author gleaned from a teaching career spanning a period from 1952 to 1987. While, for stylistic reasons, I have elected to write mostly in the present tense, I make absolutely no claim to represent an accurate picture of these schools as they are now. Indeed, from reading their bulletins and magazines, it is already evident to me that many of the problems I discuss in the pages that follow already are being addressed by some of the schools in my sample. I do know from my questionnaires, interviews, and conversations with prep school colleagues over the years that many share the perceptions related in the pages of this book. Others, I am equally certain, do not. I beg those in the latter group who may be displeased with what I say here to remember that perceptions are only that: views of reality, rather than reality itself. I further urge those who find themselves in this latter group not to be satisfied with merely believing that my perceptions are wrong. Instead, I hope they will go on to ask how a person like myself, who has been in these schools for so long, as well as so many of the well-meaning students and faculty in my study, could share these perceptions. So doing leads to cooperative efforts toward making the schools we have all loved and served as good as they can possibly be.

Barbara Bernache-Baker, Ph.D.
Vieques, Puerto Rico
December 2000

TABLE OF CONTENTS

INTRODUCTION

"Boy, I had no idea the preppy problem had gotten so out of hand."

"The Governor's doing the right thing. Statewide aerial spraying is the only solution."

— G.B. Trudeau, *Doonesbury*

In the mid-1980s the *Boston Globe* reported an assault on a female boarding student at a New England college preparatory school by a male boarding student at the same school. According to the *Globe*, the headmaster would confirm only that an "incident" had occurred and that two students had been expelled. Over the next few days more details came to light, and the *Globe* reported that seven male students were expelled and eight others less severely disciplined.

According to the headmaster (as quoted in the *Globe*), a female student and a male student had been drinking "large quantities" of vodka in the woods near the school. The students returned to their respective dormitories before the 10:20 p.m. bed check. The boy later left his dormitory and went to the girl's room, where she had passed out, and had sexual intercourse with her. On returning to his dormitory, he bragged to his roommate about his "sexual conquest." One source related that the boy's peers questioned the veracity of his story. In response, the boy returned to the girl and carried her, clad only in her pajama top, back to his room. His roommate then proceeded to race around the dormitory, telling other students. Several arrived on the scene and encouraged the boy and his roommate to "sexually fondle" the girl, making "insulting and demeaning suggestions and comments" to her. Only later did some students intervene and return the young woman to her dormitory.

Far more than in almost any other human culture, Western society in general and the United States in particular have placed value-based rules on sexual attitudes and behavior with an eye, it is usually stated, toward the betterment of both the individual and society. We have done so to such an extent that the study of the sexual behavior of any one group often reveals much about the value system within which the individuals composing that group developed. Furthermore, in these days of feminist consciousness, it is probably not necessary to elaborate on a point made several times by contemporary writers over the past few years, that views of sex and sexuality often reflect values involved in the formation of political opinions.

If true for individuals, it is no less true for institutions. In this case, the institutions are college preparatory schools claiming to play a major role in shaping the values of those who attend them. The result, it is implied, distinguishes their graduates from students who attended a public school. I therefore elected to use the area of human sexuality to see if significant differences between the value-based attitudes and behavior of the students who had attended prep schools and their public school counterparts actually exist. My results, plus additional information gathered from confidential interviews with students, faculty, and staff at the 16 college preparatory schools involved in my study, led me to the uncomfortable feeling that the aforementioned sexual exploitation incident might just as well have occurred at any other such school.

I started this research recognizing there were two possible outcomes. One was that statistically significant differences would, indeed, be found between the two groups. The other was that no such differences existed. If the first turned out to be correct, it would enable me to hypothesize some possible causes for these differences. For example, if it is true in our society that money equals power, then parental income might influence sexual attitudes and behavior. College preparatory school tuition and room-and-board often are extremely high (from $6,000 to more than $12,000 per year at the time I did my research in the 1980s, and almost certainly far more than that today). For this reason, prep schools have traditionally served a population of adolescents who, in general, represent the most affluent segment of American society. Considering the economically advantageous surroundings in which a prep school student's mind develops, one might expect differences in attitudes and behavior. There are other possible explanations, of course. It might be that the intense academic pressure found in college preparatory schools influences sexual attitudes and behavior. Furthermore, prep school students usually live at their schools, often long distances from their homes. Perhaps spending these critical adolescent years away from home influences sexual attitudes and behavior. On the other hand, the absence of a significant difference in attitudes and behavior also would be of interest because many schools claim to promote such differences and many parents have been led to expect them.

And parents do expect these schools to instill values. For example, one New England prep school was sued by an irate parent whose son was involved with drugs at the school.

Another example involved the brutal beating of a male student at Deerfield Academy by six other students (four of the students were expelled and two suspended). The school's stated mission is "To educate young people — intellectually, esthetically, socially, physically, and morally — so that they become responsible, contributing citizens and fulfilled human beings." One irate parent was quoted in the New York Daily News (12 November 2000): "I left my child in their care . . . I feel he was let down and got caught up in a mob mentality. He was a boy who had everything going for him, a top student, and now he feels like his life is ruined. These schools need to be on top of this." To his credit, Deerfield head Eric Widmer avoided simple damage control and admitted that the incident was part of a pattern of bullying at Deerfield. In a letter to the parents of all Deerfield students, Widmer wrote that "even at Deerfield, where we talk so much about mutual respect and human decency, we are not immune to such episodes and that otherwise fine students are not immune to cruel impulses."

My findings did not support the prep schools' claims to moral superiority. In most of the attitudes and behavior areas in which values clearly seem to be involved, there were no statistically significant differences between college preparatory school and college-bound public school graduates. Far more discouraging was the list of behaviors and attitudes in which significant differences *were* found. For example, sexual activity is the prep school's bugaboo, and a great deal of time and effort is devoted to preventing it. Yet, despite all these precautions (often involving a vast expenditure of faculty energy) no less than two-thirds of the prep school students in my sample had had sexual intercourse by graduation, as compared to less than half of their public school counterparts.

Alcohol and drug use by students is another issue that often causes sleepless nights for headmasters and faculty. Yet, despite round-the-clock policies of an intensity not possible at public schools, far more alcohol and drug use occurred among prep school students than among public school students, much of it accompanied by sexual activity. Most discouraging of all, with or without drugs, sexual activity among prep school students was generally of a non-caring, highly exploitative nature. I hope in the pages that follow to suggest reasons why these schools, despite all their wonderful resources and potential, seem to be failing in this area.

It should be kept in mind that these are college-bound students. When I compared my entire study sample with Sorensen's nationwide probability sample of high school-age adolescents, there were significant differences (see Appendix). But when I compared my sample with Sorensen's college-bound prep school and public school students, these differences largely disappeared. That suggests that the attitudes and behaviors of college-bound students are considerably different from those of other students.

Much of what I found was neither what I expected nor what I wished. This led to some hard thinking and to carrying out a careful review of what the sample prep school students had written on their anonymous questionnaires or said in their personal and confidential interviews. I needed to know why these young people viewed themselves and their schools in the way that they did. Therefore I randomly sampled faculty members of the 16 college preparatory schools involved in my study — one out of four at the larger schools and one out of two at the smaller. I wanted to determine faculty perceptions of their schools' philosophies, especially in comparison to their own individual value systems.

The results of this follow-up work with the faculty were even more shocking to me. I had expected considerable differences between faculty and student views concerning school rules and policies, and these did appear. However, to an absolutely astounding degree, both students and faculty perceived their schools as publicly proclaiming one set of values while privately practicing other values. This perceived difference in public and private values extended beyond values relating to human sexuality to include such areas as faculty salaries, gender equality, academics versus athletics, and respect for individual rights and differences. These and other issues are discussed in the pages that follow.

For those not of the college preparatory school world, Chapters 1, 2, and 3 provide a brief overview of these institutions from a historical, administrative, and faculty-staff perspective. Next follow chapters on religion and athletics, two areas of prep school life that reveal much about the schools' self-image and value systems. Values are also a central part of the following chapters dealing with sexuality, quite possibly the most value-laden of all activities in Western cultures, and the way these values extend to perceptions of gender and sexual preference differences.

I end with my own personal reflections on my research in the light of many years of prep school teaching. Much of what I have to say will hardly be pleasing to the administrators or some of my former faculty colleagues at these schools. However, I wish to stress that I have had no desire other than to produce a book that will be helpful, rather than destructive, to their vitally important mission. College preparatory schools should be encouraged in their current efforts to move from the elitist status they once enjoyed toward applying the very considerable skills and resources they have always possessed to the pressing social issues of our time.

In those chapters dealing with my research, I have included direct quotes from my student and faculty samples. It is my strong feeling that these quotes convey their respective messages far more effectively than could data tables or paraphrasing. In this context, it is important to stress that, unless otherwise specified, these quotes represent statistically significant majority opinions; I merely took the liberty of selecting those that, to me, expressed those opinions most powerfully.

No person writes in a vacuum. Therefore it might be helpful for the reader to know something about my own background, for I would be the last to deny that my perceptions must almost certainly be a product of it.

First, though I certainly had no inkling of it at the time, my earliest educational experiences taught me what an education should very definitely *not* be. As a Roman Catholic in the pre-Vatican II days, attendance at a parochial school was usually expected and, at times, even enforced. Though raised in Windsor, Connecticut, the home of the Loomis Chaffee School, there was no question of my ever going there. Instead, I attended Mount St. Joseph Academy in West Hartford (now closed), thus missing out on the superior education that "that *Protestant* school!" clearly afforded.

Precisely the same reasoning prevailed in the choice of college. Though accepted at Smith College, it was deemed proper that I attend an absolutely *atrocious* Roman Catholic women's college in Vermont. Here my biology textbook included a section on the thoughts of St. Augustine, along with frequent discourses on the biological basis for such matters as the sacramental nature of marriage! Among the nuns then composing the vast majority of the faculty, some had only bachelor degrees and only one had her doctorate (in Latin). The only other faculty possessing doctoral degrees were those brought in from the secular world — quite possibly a necessity if the college was to remain accredited.

In *The Smoke of Satan* (1999) Fordham University professor of sociology and anthropology Michael W. Cuneo referred to the attempts to improve things in the Catholic education system of those days as "rare shafts of light upon an otherwise bleak intellectual landscape" and cites the observation of historian John Tracy Ellis that "Catholic higher education of the day was distinguished by formalism, moralism, and authoritarianism — qualities hardly conducive to the pursuit of intellectual excellence."

In such an education atmosphere, it is not surprising that, according to the class notes in my college alumnae newsletter, other than entering convents, the main accomplishments of the graduates of those days seemed to be producing children (though goodness knows the college spared no efforts to prevent us from learning *how*!). When I look at my yearbook and recall some of the ridiculous rules and activities to which we were all subjected, I wonder what sort of women we must have been to have permitted it.

Toward the end of my undergraduate years, three very fortunate things happened that made an otherwise intellectually unrewarding period of my life worthwhile. For one, despite strong disapproval, I began dating a Chinese man (the nuns referred to him as "that *Heathen*"), a biology major attending the University of Vermont. From him, I learned much of the basic subject matter of biology I should have been learning at my college. Second, through this man I met a friend of his at UVM who, five years later, would become my husband. Third, I was fortunate enough to attract the attention of Elsa Sichel, a scientist brought in from the outside, secular world to teach a few biology courses. Though Dr. Sichel could hardly be described as an inspiring teacher, she did treat students as individuals whose ideas were worthy of respect in their own right. Through her I obtained a research position with the late Henry Crosby Stetson at Harvard University's Museum of Comparative Anatomy and the Woods Hole Oceanographic Institute in Massachusetts.

It was at Harvard and Woods Hole that my real education began. Here I experienced for the first time the genuine intellectual excitement of research and learning for learning's sake, unencumbered with any one philosophical view.

Interestingly, Cushing Academy's retiring head, Joseph R. Curry, who was a colleague of mine on the Mount Hermon faculty, experienced the same feeling as I did at Harvard after his experiences at a military college. In the Spring 2000 issue of his school's magazine, *Cushing*, he notes: "Harvard was without question the most important educating experience of my life. In many ways it was the exact opposite of the Citadel. Harvard valued the intellect and pursuit of knowledge. It valued ideals and values that were humane. I can't imagine accomplishing anything that I may have accomplished in my life without having had the experience of Harvard."

That Curry and I experienced the same intellectual liberation at Harvard is, of course, purely coincidental. I am sure that he would agree that it could have occurred just as easily at any other academically excellent liberal arts college. However, it was at Harvard and in my later years of graduate study elsewhere that I had a chance to study the historical origins of the various teachings which, at my college, were presented to us as inviolable "Truths," with a capital T, not subject to questioning. Gradually, I came to see how the immense power of education is like a double-edged sword that may be swung in two ways, one so as to repress and control, the other to liberate and affirm. It is the latter which a liberal arts education is all about, and it is the latter to which we in college preparatory schools are supposed to be providing an introduction. It was in the context of this conviction that I approached the writing of this book.

CHAPTER 1

The Prep School in Historical Perspective

"The school will provide efficient teaching, manly discipline, and systematic exercise and association with boys of purpose."
— George C. St. John, Headmaster, Choate, 1908–1947

No institution can be understood divorced from the context of its historical development, and the New England college preparatory school is certainly no exception. Regretfully, it lies beyond the scope and intent of this book to provide anything more than a sketchy (though, I believe, not inaccurate) picture. I refer the interested reader to some of the works referenced throughout this book for a more thorough treatment.

In the United States we have become accustomed to at least try to educate all of our citizens at either public or private expense. Historically, however, education was strictly for the elite, who recognized that knowledge and power go hand in hand. An intricate weave of academic scholarship and "right" or "moral" thinking was viewed as the proper mental tapestry for those who would later possess political, social, and religious power.

College education in the United States began as an elitist, male-dominated enterprise with strong moral overtones. The highly secular image they convey today obscures the fact that such universities as Harvard, Yale, and Princeton began as essentially religious institutions, lacing the education they provided with a

Christian view. It was the graduates of such institutions who founded many New England college preparatory schools, and still more such graduates, of considerable financial means, who funded them. Thus the historical development of these prep schools parallels that of the prestigious colleges and universities to which they would send their graduates. From the start, prep schools were intended to serve an elitist clientele and to teach elitist social skills and philosophies; private school graduates would later take over their parents' money, power, and position. So, too, would many of the power elite of the corporate, financial, and political ranks come from the prep school world. It is no accident, for example, that buildings on the campuses of some New England college preparatory schools bear such names as Carnegie, Mellon, and Rockefeller.

This is not to claim that all students who attend prep schools today come from an elitist socioeconomic group. However, prep school students and their parents do represent a more affluent and better-educated portion of our society. Furthermore, with their concentration on molding a very intense education environment laced strongly with a moralistic view, prep schools at times give the impression of having progressed only a little beyond the stance they held years ago. They still are perceived by those who are not a part of their world, as well as by many who actually attend or who work in them, as being very far from egalitarian.

In this context, it is pertinent to mention here Peter Cookson and Caroline Hodges Persell's *Preparing for Power* (1985), a study involving a far larger number of college preparatory schools than did mine.* While the study is interesting in its own right, the

---

*I limited my own research to college preparatory schools in New England. For historical reasons, this region is the center for most of the high-quality college preparatory schools. Institutions such as Choate (now Choate–Rosemary Hall), Deerfield, Groton, Phillips Andover, Phillips Exeter, St. Paul's, and so on, have for years set a standard for academic excellence that many prep schools located elsewhere in the country attempt to emulate. Thus I proceeded on the assumption that it made sense to use those institutions that exemplify the prep school world; and with some notable exceptions (the Hill School in Pennsylvania and Lawrenceville in New Jersey, for example) these are found in New England. Cookson and Persell's research was nationwide in scope.

reactions to it were still more so. One of the headmasters under whom I served took pen in hand to attack the book in his school magazine, labeling it a "virulent and tendentious polemic." Yet at the same time, he admitted that the authors were "accurate and fair in presenting the excellent educational programs of these schools and in showing their success in preparing their students for college placement." If Cookson and Persell are accurate and fair when praising the schools, why are they biased when critical? Interestingly, synonymous with writing his critique of Cookson and Persell, this same headmaster had read and approved for distribution a fundraising memo that was the epitome of the materialistic elitism that Cookson and Persell maintain still characterizes many schools and to which this headmaster took exception. And this headmaster was by no means alone. A lengthy review of *Preparing for Power* appeared in the official journal of the National Association of Independent Schools, an organization to which many independent schools belong. The author, Arthur G. Powell, described Cookson and Persell's effort as "a rousing, hyperbolic, sometimes flippant assault on boarding schools," and found Cookson and Persell's research had "scholarly inadequacies" (1986).

Although Powell's article makes some valid and important points, they become lost in what appear as desperate efforts to convince the reader that Cookson and Persell were wrong. In fact, all Cookson and Persell were saying was that, despite the egalitarian image they now attempt to portray, prep schools still possess strong elements of the clubby, wealth-oriented elitism that they once proudly advertised and often, sub rosa, still promote. The prep school graduates in my sample identified strongly with the picture of their schools painted by Cookson and Persell, as did many faculty members. It was rather ironic to see prep school representatives protesting Cookson and Persell's suggestion that their schools prepare their students for wielding political or economic power when the schools' own promotional magazines generally contain articles proudly featuring graduates who have done or are doing just that. It was for the social acceptability and contacts that might enable them to attain such power that Joseph Kennedy chose to send his sons Joseph and John F. to Choate, rather than to the parochial schools that would have been the logical choice for an Irish Catholic family of that day.

In truth, the democratization of today's prep schools is probably more the result of changes in the demographics of the student bodies over the past two or three decades than anything else. Jews and Catholics, once distinctly in the minority, are now found in large numbers on most prep school campuses. Chapel services, if held at all, no longer present only a Protestant (usually Episcopalian) or even a Christian view. This broadening of viewpoint has immeasurably enriched the intellectual climate at the schools.

As student demographics go, so also go those of the faculty. While precise figures are difficult to obtain, it would be surprising not to find both Jews and Catholics well represented on the faculties of the leading New England college preparatory schools today. However, to the best of my knowledge, at only one of the schools in my study has a person born a Jew or Roman Catholic ever been head. The single case, a Roman Catholic, was a person who, though of a spiritual bent, by his own admission was not actively practicing his faith.

The same is true concerning the minority presence among students and faculty. While major changes have occurred, these schools are still a very long way from being representative of our society as a whole. The initial presence of black and Latino students was often the result of social forces generated by the civil rights movements of the 1950s and 1960s. Individuals or families of different cultures might be brought to campus in various capacities depending on which minority was "in vogue." Over the years, at four different schools, I have seen Puerto Ricans, Africans, Hungarians (former "Freedom Fighters" of the 1956 Soviet Union occupation), Vietnamese, and so forth, brought to New England campuses as scholarship students, faculty members, or, in one case, the school physician. From what I observed over the years I taught, the results of bringing persons from faraway places to the often shockingly different environment of a New England prep school campus were sometimes benign and occasionally helpful. At others, they merely showed differences between value systems and cultural mores — valuable for the American prep school students, if not always so for the foreign students.

A story widely circulated on the Mount Hermon campus during the 1950s was that of a coach observing a newly admitted African student on the athletic fields throwing a javelin. Meaning to be helpful, the coach informed the student that he would never get any distance holding the javelin as he was. The reported reply was: "Me not throw for distance — me throw for accuracy." Treated as a joke then, the incident would be treated more accurately today as symbolizing deep cultural differences to be bridged.

During the days of "Papa Doc" Duvalier, my husband and I became good friends with a Haitian refugee who came to our school to teach French. According to one of his colleagues, he could not speak that language correctly and his English was equally deficient, therefore the situation became a disastrous one for his students. Furthermore, his habitual use of garlic, both internally and externally (he hung a bag of crushed garlic around his neck) for health reasons, made him an unlikely person to approach for extra help. His personal life also hardly squared with the life extolled by the school; his residence often was frequented by women of extraordinary beauty and questionable occupation. This faculty member's presence on campus created a situation that the school found itself entirely incapable of handling. To fire him would, for obvious reasons, have been bad publicity for the school. The problem was solved only by his death.

Lest the preceding examples appear entirely cynical, I hasten to assure the reader that this is not my intent. Rather, it is to remind us of biologist Garrett Hardin's ecological dictum: "We can never do just one thing." However well-meaning, our actions have effects that are not always as beneficial as we imagine, and which may even be tragic. The 1960s taught us much about white liberal guilt. This guilt has led us to actions that, if nothing else, revealed us to be as capable of ethnic insensitivity as are the most blatant bigots.

From my experience, sporadic causes, undertaken as "world food hunger" or "nuclear weapon awareness" days, serve mainly as a salve for the consciences of those involved, rather than as a serious way of addressing issues. Such superficial activities encourage students to apply ineffectual bandages to deeply rooted infections and create the self-delusion of having taken genuine steps toward a cure. With the best of intentions, faculty may use the power of their position to make *their* pet causes those of their students. However, faculty and students often perceive matters quite differently. In his discussion of race relations, Sizer makes this point quite succinctly:

> One leaves visits to dozens of American high schools with the clear feelings . . . that race is a fixation of adults more than of the young and that class differences mean much more among adolescents. Again, class and race often overlap and affect one another. But the operative issues for students arise more from class behavior than from skin color. In America's paradoxical focus on race to obliterate racism, we may make more of it than it deserves. Awareness, fairness, yes, obsession, no. But at the same time, we play the class issue at low volume. Americans find it embarrassing. The poor adolescent scrambles into adulthood, often taking risks and responsibilities never faced by his or her more affluent peers throughout their entire lives. Wealthier youths — the majority of the school population — have their protections built in; they are masked from many of the world's harsher realities. Because of the surroundings which forge them, modern adolescents differ more along income-class lines than along any other. (1984, p. 38)

There is considerable wisdom in this statement, especially concerning income-class lines and prep schools. As if to echo Sizer's words, Kendra Stearns O'Donnell, the former head of Phillips Exeter Academy, noted:

> I wonder. . . what we are doing within schools to empower all that diversity. I notice in my own school a tendency which may relate to your own age and state in life. . . to want to be like each other . . . to want, in fact, to all be the same

in some way. There is a norm for dress, a norm for language, a norm for behavior and there are along with that norm what one student at Exeter told me are "the haves and have nots." But the "have nots" are very aware of wanting to be "haves" and this has much more to do with lots of different cultural things, not just Rolex watches. I think the real challenge, if we are going to make diversity count as it should in our schools, is to find ways to keep the diversity alive once it enters our gates. . . . I think the minority experience and the experience of diversity in general is apt to be one of the most distinguishing things about boarding schools *if we let it be.* (1996, emphasis added)

CHAPTER 2

Prep School Administration

"In part, what makes heads able to cope with the complexities of their position is that they are individuals whose perceptions of the world around them are somewhat limited."
— Cookson and Persell, *Preparing for Power*, p. 122

The administrative structures of the New England college preparatory schools with which I am familiar are patterned after the colleges and universities they emulate and to which they wish to send their students. Thus one finds such administrative positions as dean of students and dean of the faculty (generally held by a former teacher), treasurer (a position usually held by a professional administrator) and, of course, alumni director. Outside the administrative offices, a structure similar to that of a college or university also is evident, with a board of trustees being the ultimate, though not immediate, source of power. Nonadministrative faculty are divided into their various academic departments.

Even in physical appearance, most prep schools are more similar to colleges than to high schools. The campuses of such prep schools as Loomis Chaffee, Hotchkiss, Northfield Mount Hermon, Phillips Academy, Andover, or St. Paul's, for example, far surpass those of many colleges both in size and beauty. (They often do so in wealth, too. On a per capita basis, St. Paul's School is said to have endowment assets averaging $433,000 per student and has been described as wealthier than Smith College, Dartmouth, and Brown University combined.)

When one looks at the origins of most prep schools, this similarity to colleges is hardly surprising. Their founders often specifically planned for them to resemble certain select, usually Ivy League, colleges and universities. These founders wanted to create an environment to which their students would become adapted and therefore one in which they might desire to continue after graduation.

Despite these similarities, there are two highly significant differences that separate colleges from college preparatory schools. The first is that the former deal with young adults, the latter with adolescents. This crucial difference always must be considered when comparing the two kinds of institutions. The second difference is more pertinent here: While colleges and universities have presidents, college preparatory schools have headmasters, headmistresses, or some other term designating this position.

In the past (and still in some schools) male faculty members were called "masters."* Thus the term *headmaster* simply denoted the higher position of authority. And it is a higher position. Groton graduate John Sedgwick describes headmaster William Polk as follows:

> his sky blue eyes, set deep in their sockets, can pierce you, and his bass voice resonates with an impassioned fervor as he speaks with the greater truths that Groton has always espoused. At Groton, the Rector (author's note: Groton founder and first headmaster, Endicott Peabody) is still God, and Polk is his prophet. (1988, p. 109)

Similarly, Hotchkiss School board of trustees president Frank Sprole (Class of 1938), writes of the experience of a student arriving at a boarding school for the first time as one of becoming "a citizen of a different country" and simultaneously entering into "an unfamiliar and exotic culture, complete with confusing

---

*The term *headmaster* was matched in all-female prep schools by the term *headmistress*. For obvious reasons, the female counterpart for "masters" was never used. The gender-free term, *head*, now is used generally to replace *headmaster* and *headmistress*. For my purposes here, where appropriate, I use the more traditional *headmaster* or simply *head*.

tribal customs and odd lingo." He then describes the role and nature of the headmaster:

> there in the middle of this mystifying and intimidating civilization stands a single figure, the headmaster, the visible, living essence of the place.
>
> He may have a nickname. There may be irreverent stories about him and even more irreverent about his speech or manner — those idiosyncrasies that schoolboys take such delight in. He may be beloved or revered, or even disliked or feared. And yet — though his blazer may be worn thin at the elbows and his necktie may be unfashionably narrow or wide — there is about him what Shakespeare calls the "divinity that doth hedge a king" — and no Caesar in Rome, no Plantagenet in Whitehall, no Louis in Versailles has ever been more the undoubted monarch of all he surveys. From lordly seniors down to the humblest prep, every student is the headmaster's subject. He is the one bond they all have in common. In a sense, he is the father of them all. From that unity stems the feeling of belonging that makes a school a school. (1998, p. 21)

At most top-ranked colleges and universities, the real power is wielded by the academic departments, with the president often relegated to a figurehead or fundraiser role. Depending on his proclivities, however, the prep school headmaster rules with an iron hand or velvet glove. Whatever his mode of operating, however, rule he does. Historian Doris Kearns Goodwin describes the Choate headmaster when John F. Kennedy was a student there, George C. St. John, as a "tall, severe-looking man with hollow cheeks and a balding head" who

> presided over the students and faculty with a strong, authoritarian hand. Demanding total loyalty from his faculty, who were expected to live in houses on the campus and perform triple duty as teachers, house masters and coaches, St. John considered marriage an outside threat to the integrity of the school and required that faculty members receive his special consent if they wished to marry. (1987, p. 458)

The histories of several prep schools reveal a critical formative period in which a struggling institution emerges into a leadership role under the guidance (in truth, more often the dictatorial prodding) of a powerful headmaster. Examples include Frank Boyden at Deerfield, Endicott Peabody at Groton, and Nathaniel Horton Batchelder at Loomis (now the coeducational Loomis Chaffee School). While the choice of a new president at an institution such as Harvard University may scarcely affect the daily routine of most faculty, the appointment of a new headmaster usually directly and dramatically influences the school. The new appointment will touch virtually all personnel, and they know it. At such times, campus gossip (a central feature of all prep schools) reaches a fever pitch.

Headmastering a few decades ago often gave the appearance of a genetic basis. Brothers Elliot and Frank Speer, for example, were both headmasters of different prep schools (Mount Hermon and Loomis), and Choate's George C. St. John was succeeded by his son, the Reverend Seymour St. John. In truth, this simply reflects the degree to which a small number of persons of like social station often controlled the direction and philosophies of the leading New England college preparatory schools. Now, however, just as most colleges have moved toward a greater democratization of decision-making, so, too, have many prep schools. At these schools, the selection process for a new headmaster might involve a search or interview committee composed of members of the administration, faculty, and even students.

Historically, such democratic procedures were not the case. The power of selection lay very much in the hands of the schools' board of trustees, usually composed of "old grads" and, more often than not, led by one or two members strongly imprinted with memories of the school in "the good old days." This "imprinting" strongly influenced their choice of headmaster. The result was often the appointment of a person whose views reflected the values of yesteryear and therefore were out of phase with those of younger faculty members or students. Furthermore, because prep schools for most of their history were distinctly

WASPish, to say nothing of male-dominated, it is usual even today for these schools to be led by a head whose philosophy is probably Protestant and certainly at least Christian. While most heads and school chaplains today are educated beyond the cloddish insensitivity of finishing an evening meal's grace to a religiously heterogeneous group with an "in Jesus' name we pray," the Christian philosophical bias remains, often imparted through speeches and an alumni newsletter or magazine.

Of course, the degree to which the headmaster of a contemporary prep school actually leads is open to question. Whereas a late 19th or early 20th century headmaster could expect to be greeted with enthusiasm and support for such homilies as "how our school nurtures the development of Christian young men," today even a modernized and less explicit variation on this theme is likely to be greeted (at least privately) with more amusement than approval by students and faculty. However, it is perception rather than reality that often counts in such matters.

Like that of a college president, a headmaster's tenure at an institution is apt to be short, sometimes painfully so. Deerfield Academy's headmaster Frank Boyden's 65 years is surely a record that may never be broken; the average term for a school head today is less than seven years. Many of the headmasters I have known have held the post in at least two schools, and others seem to be constantly playing musical chairs.

Some heads, such as retiring Taft School Headmaster Lance R. Odden, are former faculty members. Most are selected from within the prep school world, gain administrative experience at the school where they taught, then generally move elsewhere to assume command. The advantage is not having to deal with former colleagues with whom one was once on equal terms. But there also are disadvantages. Many try to transform their new school into a model of the one in which they spent their formative years, either as a student or a faculty member. Because each prep school prides itself on having its own distinct traditional flavor, such efforts often are bitterly resented. Resulting dissension produces pressure that, more often than not, leads to a resignation.

As was often the case with college and university presidents, the 1960s were a difficult time for headmasters. The anti-Vietnam War and civil rights movements, combined with a strong appeal of the counterculture movement to students and young faculty, led some campuses to drop required chapel, adopt a relaxed dress code, and admit many minority students. Many older alumni, already apoplectic at the idea of their old school becoming co-educational, now gazed at photographs in the alumni magazine of long-haired male students whose coats and ties were replaced with T-shirts and blue jeans and female students who, in their eyes at least, were dressed not one bit better. Further, the students represented a range of ethnic and religious backgrounds that these alumni could scarcely have comprehended in their day. Complaints were aired (usually privately), purse strings were tightened or closed altogether, and the headmaster deemed responsible for the "slipping standards" was encouraged to go elsewhere. Certainly some of this alumni dissatisfaction did reflect sexist, racist, or elitist views. More often, however, it was nothing more than a nostalgic desire to preserve the world they knew and loved at a critical period of their lives and to which they attributed their later success.

If early headmasters played a major role in the life of the school, no less so did their wives. For each headmaster, she was his constant companion (if somewhat in the background) and community hostess for student and faculty punch-and-cookie parties at "the headmaster's house." In the days prior to coeducation, the headmaster's wife often was the only highly visible woman on an all-boys campus. She therefore often became sort of a surrogate mother to many boys, especially those homesick for their own. Perhaps it is not surprising that, despite her clearly subservient role to that of her husband, the headmaster's wife's name appears quite often in the reminiscences of older alumni.

It is in the role of headmaster's wife — surely as traditional a role as could be described for a woman — that one finds a significant change. In response to the question, "What is your perception of the role of the headmaster's wife (or headmistress' husband) at your school?" faculty answered that very few headmaster's wives play the traditional role. In fact, some had purposely rejected such a lifestyle, electing instead to lead their own independent careers, even if unrelated to the interests of the school. A few male faculty described this phenomenon in a manner that was almost petulant, as if they sensed a personal rejection of themselves or their schools. Several female faculty members, however, stated explicitly that these headmasters' wives were providing a valuable role model for both female faculty and for students.

The question purposely left open the possibility of a headmistress with a husband who filled the spouse's role. In truth, until 1987, when Phillips Exeter appointed Kendra Stearns O'Donnell (an Emma Willard School graduate) to head the school, to the best of my knowledge no such situation existed in the major New England college preparatory schools. (In 1994 Phillips Andover selected Barbara Landis Chase as school head.) It is for this reason that my discussion here is so male-oriented. Furthermore, when coeducation was achieved by the union of two campuses, in no case was the head of the all-female school put in charge. Even Cushing Academy, despite being chartered as a coeducational institution in 1865, had never had a female head. The reasons for this obvious discrimination are both complex and historical and relate strongly to prep schools' past tendencies to act as preservers of social traditions, rather than as a challenge to them.

The power wielded *sub rosa* by a headmaster often is shown by the degree to which his interests influence those of his school community. My husband and I recall an annual campaign held at Mount Hermon School during the years we taught there. Its intent was to raise funds for a small school, the Collège Cévenol in France (like Mount Hermon, founded by a Protestant evangelist), an institution with which the school had long been involved. Despite strong cheerleading by the headmaster, most of the faculty and still more of the students could have cared less, at least privately. Yet each year a communitywide campaign, led by a highly respected French teacher and lasting several days, obscured anything else of campus significance. Daily reports on the financial progress of the campaign were broadcast to the faculty and students in the school's massive dining hall. These daily reports were given in a manner that not only pitted dormitory against dormitory, but also dorm floor against dorm floor. As a result, for many the Collège Cévenol campaign became a dreaded time of the year.

Like many well-meaning programs, the results at the local level often were disastrous. "Floor officers," seniors entrusted with the care of students on their dormitory floors, found themselves charged with the responsibility of collecting from their charges. With their competitive enthusiasm fanned both by the campaign directors and by resident faculty members desirous of impressing the headmaster with their Francophilia, the line between merely collecting money and not-too-subtle extortion was easily crossed. Younger students, in particular, were easy victims; saying "no" to a husky and usually popular 18-year-old is a difficult task for one only 13 or 14, especially in the light of a "Come on, Jones, you can afford more than that," or, "Do you want second floor Crossley to beat fourth floor Overtoun?" My husband remembers encountering a tearful freshman who had money simply taken from the top of his bureau by his floor officer; because his father owned a grocery store chain, it was announced that "he could afford it." Besides, "Wasn't it for a good cause?" It took a long time for my husband to uncover the cause for the tears. The student's genuine fear of reprisal should it appear he had complained was understandable under the campus mood during Collège Cévenol campaign days. It spoke eloquently about how this headmaster's power, even in a good cause, resulted in bad effects.

Such a situation could never arise at any good college or university. Their presidents simply do not have the power and control over faculty behavior that their prep school counterparts have. College faculty know that they are professionals in their own right and use that knowledge in governing their behavior. To an absolutely astonishing degree, prep school faculty do not. Criticism of the administration at the college level tends to be open; letters from faculty members blasting this or that policy appear in the campus newspaper or are voiced openly in faculty meetings. Although I have taught under headmasters whose policies, at times, were extremely unpopular, I have *never* seen this occur at the prep school level. Instead, the criticisms remained underground, appearing only in campus gossip. This failure of prep school faculty to speak out openly seems an inevitable part of the prep school faculty psyche. In fact, the headmaster who tries to "democratize" things is most apt to be a victim of the harshest criticism for his "lack of leadership." It is as if the challenge to lead, rather than being led, creates a feeling of faculty insecurity.

There are several results of this absence of free and open discussion on prep school campuses, none of them positive. For one, it generates a lack of openness and trust between faculty; each seems to fear that a slip of the tongue in a weak moment might be used against him or her. Almost certainly, it was the anonymity provided by my survey questionnaires that led to the large number, long length, and frankness of my respondents' comments. Even in my formal and informal face-to-face interviews, fear of being identified as the source of information often surfaced. I recall vividly one interviewee being highly critical of the headmaster (mostly because he did not go to all of the athletic events). Spotting me the next day on campus after our talk, he rushed over to say that he did not want to be interpreted as being negative about the headmaster, who was really a "great guy," and to stress how very much he loved the school. I had to reassure him again of my standard promise of confidentiality. His wife, I might add, was far less afraid to speak out openly and seemed not at all worried about being identified. (In general, this was more characteristic of the women than the men I interviewed.)

Another negative result of a lack of free and open discussion at prep schools is that serious issues become submerged by the stress of preserving a school's "image." So overriding is this "image factor" in the prep school that it dominates most of the books written about prep schools. Some schools are so nervous about such issues as drugs or sex that they do not even trust their own faculty. One interviewee told me of a colleague suggesting during a faculty meeting that they discuss the problem of drugs on campus. The subject was quickly changed by the headmaster. Afterward, the head summoned the faculty member into his office to inform him, in no uncertain terms, that a faculty meeting is not an appropriate place to raise such issues. Treating faculty members as if they were children, rather than as professionals in their own right, is unfortunately quite common at prep schools. Equally unfortunate, the faculty have far too often allowed the schools to get away with it.

I recall one incident vividly. A male faculty member at one school where I taught was forced to resign. The faculty was informed only to the extent of being told that he had been "involved" with a student. Further information came out only when the student involved informed on other students and they, in turn, told faculty members. Not entrusting the faculty with as complete a disclosure as possible forced them to imagine what had happened, ranging from a kiss to sexual intercourse — with most, of course, thinking the latter. Ironically, even the purpose of the secrecy was foiled. The same day I learned of the dismissal, I attended an evening dinner and science lecture at Miss Porter's School in Farmington, Connecticut, which also was attended by science faculty from other prep schools. No sooner had I been identified by school at the dinner table than I was asked about the incident. It was only then that I first learned that the faculty member in question also had been involved previously with a student at another prep school where he had taught. My reaction to being questioned about the incident was a defensive one. Rather than responding, I was evasive and changed the subject. I acted in precisely the same manner that I had criticized. Instead of sharing my own experience and research on the subject with the other teachers at the table, I reacted defensively to protect my school's image. Faculty-student sexual relations had occurred at every prep school in which I had taught and, as I knew from my own research, in many others as well. The incident raised the question of how to deal with the very serious problem of sexual exploitation that touches every prep school, a problem that cries out for intra- and interschool cooperation. Yet, rather than share information from my own experience and research with the other teachers at the table, I reacted defensively to protect my school's image. As a supposedly professional educator, I cannot remember ever being more thoroughly ashamed of myself.

The real pity of the paternalistic aura that surrounds the headmaster position is that it encourages political sycophancy at the expense of genuine leadership. One faculty colleague for whom I had a great deal of respect underwent a complete metamorphosis on becoming a member of the administration. This former colleague completely reversed at least one previously held position to match that of the headmaster. When the headmaster joined many in criticizing Cookson and Persell's *Preparing for Power* on the ground of "poor research," this person expressed the same opinion though, when pressed, admitted to never having read the book.

Such behavior is an all-too-common theme in prep schools. It is a result of the disproportionate power of the headmaster's office. All prep school personnel are familiar with those faculty members whose main function often seems to be assuring the emperor that his new clothes are, indeed, very beautiful. Such persons, found within the inner circles of administrative power, also isolate the headmaster from the real feelings of the students and faculty.

The realization of this isolation often comes to the headmaster only when he moves elsewhere. "I never knew who our friends *weren't*," was the way one headmaster's wife put it. She was deeply hurt by the way her husband was rapidly abandoned, once his leaving became known, by those who had previously professed undying loyalty.

This theme of finding themselves undercut by former sycophants is one I have heard from other former headmasters. It reflects, I believe, the degree to which the nature of the position, far more than the nature of the individual himself, often impedes the establishment of an atmosphere characteristic of the truly excellent education communities. In this sense the Cookson and Persell statement heading this chapter is unfair — although perhaps it helps explain why so many school heads were enraged by their book. It is not the school heads I have known, nor any of those under whom I served, who were limited. Far from it. Rather it may be the way their positions have been defined historically that imposed limitations, both on them *and* their faculty members.

CHAPTER 3

Prep School Faculty and Staff

"For heads, the willingness of so many to work so hard for so little was an administrative delight. As the young triple threats aged, they either were elevated to the status of 'great teacher' or were let go. A continuous flow of youthful energy was thus ensured. A school could hum along for years staffed by hard-working, loyal teachers who asked only that they be left free to teach how they pleased, a singular reward that most heads were only too glad to grant. Teacher evaluation was conducted by rumor, gossip, how much damage there was in the dormitories they supervised, and general impressions along the grapevine. Basically you either 'fit in' (a favorite administrative phrase) or you did not."

— Cookson and Persell, *Preparing for Power,* p. 88

My husband recalls reading a study several years ago by a psychologist who listed those occupations with the highest proportion of neurotics. Prep school teachers led the list. The priesthood was second. In explaining the appearance of the priesthood, the author of the study hypothesized that the priesthood or, for that matter, the ministry in general, tends to attract insecure, "needy" persons. Such individuals, it was suggested, tend to seek reaffirmation of their own worth and therefore choose occupations promoting contact with persons whose emotional needs are even greater than their own and who will turn to them for support. The study also noted that the demands on the time of an individual priest or minister are far greater than found in most occupations.

I will deal with this "needy hypothesis" first. Not being a psychologist, I am unqualified to say to what degree it applies to prep school teachers. Most certainly it does to some. Anyone associated with prep schools for even a short time can identify faculty members who thrive on crises in which they might help; and, indeed, there are those who often look for problems so as to become involved. Furthermore, it also is not uncommon on prep school campuses to find persons in religion, either through academic departments or personal involvement, actively seeking counseling positions. This, too, lends support to the "needy hypothesis." It is interesting also to note that prep school teachers often select summer vacation occupations that place them in situations where they are once again surrogate parents, such as at summer camps.

However, it is the second comparison — demands on their time — with which all prep school teachers will wholeheartedly agree. As is often the case with the clergy, these demands come literally around the clock. As the 1986-87 Governor Dummer Academy bulletin puts it, faculty members are, to their students, "teacher, guide, counselor, advisor, coach, parent, friend." (It is typical of prep school literature to cast these roles in a moralistic light. The next sentence reads: "Consistent with this variety of roles, often held simultaneously, are the qualities of unselfishness and generosity based on a commitment to the ideals, values, and way of life of the Academy, qualities rewarded by the joy and satisfaction of sharing in the growth and maturing of young men and women.") For the time they are not on vacation, prep school teachers are without doubt among the most overworked and underpaid individuals in the United States.

The heavy demands on faculty time take several forms. Of these, classroom contact hours are the most obvious. My husband taught at a prep school for seven years. On becoming a college professor, he could hardly believe the difference. The normal course load in the sciences at his university was two courses each semester. As a prep school teacher, he taught four sections of introductory biology and one six-hour course of Advanced Placement biology throughout the year. For some teachers, the four to five sections might involve two, three, or even four different preparations, for example, French I, II, III, conversation, and literature. Unlike most good colleges, prep schools are involved in developing basic study and writing skills, and so homework is demanded along with quizzes, weekly tests, and term exams. Faculty time at home is spent grading papers and preparing for the next day's classes. While college science professors are able to turn over their laboratory sections to graduate students, prep school science teachers can rely on no more than one or two students to wash test tubes or help get out equipment. The teacher must still be present during each laboratory period.

The day's final bell brings little relief. For boarding faculty, it usually means a quick trip to the gymnasium to change into coaching clothes and two hours of further student guidance and instruction in various athletic activities. The evening meal, often taken with the students in the school dining hall, brings only the briefest respite. There usually follows an evening of being in charge of a dormitory, giving out permissions, helping with homework, dealing with homesickness or excessive noise during study hours, illness, and so on. When one adds to this the faculty and departmental meetings, duties as faculty advisors, and one or two extracurricular activities, such as the debating team, chess club, band (activities which, along with athletic events, may require trips to other schools), it becomes less unbelievable that a psychologist might find many prep school teachers neurotic. In fact, it is far more of a wonder that most of them are not raving lunatics.

It is true that prep school teachers have the advantage of long vacations as opposed to the standard two or three weeks with pay. Besides the three months of summer, there are up to two weeks at Christmas and another 10 days or so in the spring. Furthermore, unlike the college teacher who shares similar breaks, there is no pressure to use this time in scholarly research or writing. (This in itself presents another serious problem that I will discuss shortly.)

Yet another dramatic difference between prep school and college life is illustrated by the degree to which a faculty member's duties become involved with his or her students' personal lives. My husband was elected Senior Fellow of East College, a dormitory complex at Wesleyan University to which 30 or so faculty members were selected by the students as "Fellows" to share weekly meals, conversation, and an after-dinner lecture. He would occasionally visit students in the dormitory and rapidly came to disregard the odor of burning marijuana, as well as the one or two copulations stumbled on accidentally. At his prep school, on the other hand, his duty on making such a discovery was clear. In a similar vein, one leading New England prep school discovered to its horror that the headmaster had a predilection for women, both students and faculty. The case is less interesting here as an example of faculty and student sexual interaction than for providing yet another major difference between the prep school and college world. The headmaster in question had come from an Ivy League college, where his reputation as a womanizer was widely known. To the college, however, this fact was unrelated to his professional competence, which they rated highly. Thus the information about his personal life, deemed irrelevant by the college, was unfortunately not provided to the school.

At the prep school level there often is close faculty involvement with parents. While a college professor may meet his or her students' families only at commencement, the prep school teacher often gets to know the students' parents very well. Throughout the academic year, most prep schools schedule days when parents may come to the schools to talk directly with their offspring's teachers; and it is understood that the teachers are available to them at other times as well. The practice is an extraordinarily effective one in helping teachers better understand and deal with their students, but it is yet another straw on a camel's back. Especially in recent years, parents have become an increasing problem for faculty. With education viewed quite correctly as a vital ingredient for future success, prep schools, with their high academic standards, become an increasingly attractive option for parents ambitious for their children to "get ahead." Because the cost of such an education often matches or exceeds that of many colleges, the financial burden may cause intense psychological pressure on the children to "get the most out of it" (translation: "*Get high grades!*"). Thus to the trauma always attendant on the rapid physiological changes accompanying adolescence is added an often crushing burden of living up to parental expectations. The results are several, none particularly pleasant. They may range from a student's escape into lethargy (often drug-related), nervous exhaustion, or behavior patterns immature for his or her age to, far more tragic, intense hatred for one or both parents. Suicides also are well known.

Faculty salaries today present one of the greatest problems in maintaining the academic excellence for which prep schools have long been famous. The salary of prep school teachers is generally several thousand dollars lower than those of their public school counterparts. (One of my colleague's told me that his children were considered eligible for their public school's free lunch program because the family cash income fit the definition of the poverty level.) Understandably, prep schools counter publicity concerning their low salaries by pointing out that, for on-campus resident faculty at least, major living expenses are provided by the school. It is true. While at Cushing Academy, for example, I lived in a dormitory. I was therefore spared the major costs of a home mortgage, taxes, heating, maintenance, and so forth. I ate all of my meals in the school dining room. Because I could walk to almost any place I might want to go during the school day, I put minimal mileage on my car. Thus my salary, pathetic as it was, was almost entirely available for purchases other than basic necessities. Remaining an unmarried faculty member or marrying a person who also is a prep school teacher (which, as in my own case, often happens), allows one to nestle into the cocoon of a nice, secure community, one virtually ideal for raising a family.

Such security is deceptive, however. With so little actual cash flowing into the prep school teacher's pocket, he or she often must rely on an outside income (for example, a military pension or an inheritance) in order to build equity in the outside world. Whereas persons in most professions are able to bequeath to their children a reasonable estate, many prep school teachers are fortunate if they manage to accumulate enough savings for a small cabin for summer use — and even then it is usually because both spouses have worked. I became rapidly aware of this problem of equity accumulation during the few years I spent outside of the prep school world doing biological research and rearing children on the Wesleyan University campus. But it was not until I began teaching again at Loomis Chaffee that the financial naiveté of the prep school faculty world became most evident to me. At the time, Loomis Chaffee was somewhat unusual in that about 20% of the faculty were day teachers, rather than almost all boarding, as is the case at most of the better-known New England college preparatory schools. The boarding faculty often were jealous of day faculty who, because they were hired almost exclusively as teachers, were able to leave campus when classes ended and go home, free of the hectic pace of after-class athletics, dormitory duty, and the like. The day faculty, on the other hand, coveted the snug security of their boarding colleagues, most of whom seemed protected from the economic reality of life in the outside world.

That economic reality is faced in its cruelest form at retirement. Retired faculty often find themselves unable to afford the high cost of heating New England homes. They must therefore move away from the region where they have lived most of their lives. I have known of faculty members of many years' service who ended their days living in mobile homes or state-run nursing homes. Such situations stand in stark contrast to constant prep school claims to respect the worth and dignity of every individual.

Ironically, the introduction of one of the more important faculty benefits brought economic reality home to some of my boarding faculty colleagues. A few prep schools have sabbatical programs, allowing a faculty member to have a year off with pay after a certain number of years of service. As with college and universities, the time off is *intended* to be used for further study, writing, or some other form of intellectual enrichment. Yet many boarding faculty, having reached sabbatical eligibility, discover to their horror that they cannot afford to take it. With their meager salaries, they have simply not been able to save enough to cover even one year's off-campus living expenses. (One, who took a sabbatical to write a book, informed me that he found himself eligible for food stamps.) Most faculty, therefore, take other options offered by the school. At Loomis Chaffee, another option was a travel grant, amounting essentially to two bonus vacations with extra pay. This option was a distinctly mixed blessing. It was more attractive than the sabbatical. Thus the enticement for faculty to choose the latter option for furthering intellectual growth and keeping current in their academic field all too often became lost for the very campus-bound faculty who needed it most. Especially in such areas as science, where obsolescence can occur within only a year or two, this issue of the faculty keeping up to date is a crucial one for the prep school. It is possible — indeed, for economic reasons, quite common — to hire a prep school teacher with no more than a bachelor's degree in the field he or she will be teaching.

Concerning teaching competence, I have long had very strong reservations about the "professional education" courses required for public school teaching certification. My experience and that of my husband has been that the emphasis of such courses on *how* one teaches greatly limits the time for achieving competence concerning *what* one is supposed to be qualified to teach. On the other hand, their insistence on practice teaching does allow for at least some weeding out of persons who simply lack the ability to communicate. Not requiring certification, prep schools often play a sort of Russian roulette with their newly hired faculty — or, perhaps better stated, with the students these new teachers will teach. In my many years of teaching, I have seen absolute disasters in the classroom, resulting in upset students and understandably angry parents who thought they were paying good money to get good teaching. For many parents, it comes as quite a shock to find that, far from a Mr. Chips, their children may well be taught by a teacher only a few years older than they (and, occasionally, not much more mature), with little or no teaching experience. Headmaster John Rae notes that more often than not, incompetent teachers are protected by the head's reluctance to act. The single most damning criticism of headmasters and headmistresses is that they fail to dismiss teachers they know to be incompetent. . . . I can think of no other walk of life, except perhaps the ordained ministry of the Church of England, in which it is possible for a lazy man to get away with so little for so long. (1987, p. 213)

The situation is further complicated by the fact that some of the best prep school teachers began their careers in this manner. I know few teachers, prep school or public, who would ever want to repeat their first two or so years of teaching. Most certainly I would not. Therefore, the prep school usually sticks with the individual for at least two or three years, hoping for the best, before he or she is asked to go elsewhere. In the meantime, however, many students have not learned very much biology, French I, English composition, or whatever the subject may happen to be.

The personal lives of young, single prep school faculty members is especially like life in a fishbowl, on view to students, colleagues, and the administration. The administration tends to treat faculty members more as children than as responsible adults. To protect the school's image, they may be subjected to ridiculous and often degrading rules. Entertaining members of the opposite sex in dormitory apartments is usually frowned on, and overnight stays are generally forbidden. The result is to encourage devious behavior. One of my faculty colleagues, whose friend visited often, demanded and received off-campus school housing, the unstated reason being so he could stay with her on weekends. When they married, they were allowed to move back on campus. At Cushing Academy I recall that a male colleague and I used to enjoy going to a Swedish steam bath in nearby Fitchburg, where we could relax and allow the steam to relieve the week's tensions. Even this healthy, most innocent of pleasures would have been an anathema to the school. On returning to the dormitory, therefore, we would make up some excuses for our damp hair. In those mid-1950s, I could not smoke or drink in my room; when my husband (then my fiancé) would visit, he could not come to my room but was restricted to a well-chaperoned downstairs parlor. We were lucky in knowing one young married faculty couple who would let us use their apartment for privacy. The rest of the time, however, we had to drive elsewhere where we would not be seen. One even felt guilty going out for a beer.

My second faculty position was at the Mount Hermon School for Boys and the Northfield School for Girls (I taught at both schools). My husband and I had inherited from his parents the habit of having a glass of sherry before dinner — we could not then afford anything stronger. But even in the privacy of our own apartment, this was considered unacceptable behavior; and we were thought by our friends to be quite daring. One evening while entertaining faculty friends for dinner, the headmaster arrived for an unannounced social visit, a school custom then viewed as comparable to a visit by the bishop to a local vicar. As my husband greeted the headmaster at the door, one of our friends hastily shoved the sherry bottle under the sofa and the glasses were whisked away.

I look back on these and other incidents with little pride. We had succumbed to the school's pressure to preserve an image rather than defending our own individuality and basic right to lead our private lives as we wished. In so doing, we were poor role models for our students. In fact, we learned later that this headmaster, too, enjoyed a sherry hour (privately), though the "sherry" was of a far stronger, distilled variety. Indeed, one of the few results of my faculty survey that did *not* surprise me was the overwhelming number who felt, even today, that prep school faculty have to lead two lives: a "normal" one off campus and a conforming one on campus. As many of my respondents pointed out, this stultifying conformity stood in stark and hypocritical contrast to their schools' claim to show respect for the individuality of each person.

In *Preparing for Power*, Cookson and Persell state, "Almost everyone who teaches in prep schools could be doing something else" (1985, p. 85). This is probably the point in their study with which I find my sharpest disagreement. In my experience, with notable exceptions, most boarding prep school teachers could do little else. The reason has far less to do with competence than psyche. Even among those whose academic skills have remained sufficiently up-to-date to survive in the outside world, few will ever try to do so. The paternalistic, family-like atmosphere of the prep school campus provides a security blanket that few are able to discard; like Linus in the *Peanuts* cartoon strip, they would be lost without it. The written and unwritten school rules governing faculty behavior treat them as children and, by allowing it, they often become so. As headmaster Rae notes:

> The teaching staff are ambivalent about the headmaster's power. They want him to be a strong leader because that makes them feel secure but it satisfies their envy of his pre-eminence to see him momentarily unsure of himself. (1987, p. 209)

As pleasant as the surroundings of a prep school campus may be, the mindset of the school community often becomes incredibly ingrown. Major issues for daily discussion are far more apt to deal with campus politics, the latest pregnancy, who is going to get whose house, or who won the latest football game or track meet than with substantive issues of the world outside the ivy-covered walls. As one of my prep school teacher-reviewers of this book's manuscript put it:

> I agree with your point about ingrown mindset. I remember being unable, despite real efforts, to keep a conversation off students or other issues at school for more than one-half hour whenever a group of faculty was together. Much of this, I think, comes from the intensity of school life. Since one seldom leaves campus and is always involved with students, the rest of the world seems unreal, certainly not immediately important.

It was in the choice of issues for conversations among faculty that my husband and I found the biggest difference between the prep school and university faculty social environments.

Doubtless part of the absence of scholarly discourse among prep school teachers is that there is virtually no pressure on prep school faculty to engage in scholarly research and often little reward for further graduate study. As fine as most of the head-masters I have worked under have been, I have witnessed only one or two to use the power of their office in any significant way to encourage faculty intellectual growth as a curative for stagnation. One, in particular, was a master psychologist. During the years of the "new math," when there was much ferment in pre-college mathematics content and teaching techniques, this head-master expressed in a faculty meeting his pleasure at the way our science department was keeping up to date. He then went on to say that "good old _____," chairman of the mathematics department, was "lighting a fire" under his teachers, too. In truth, as everyone knew, "good old _____" had not tried anything new in the past 20 years, much less lit fires to get anyone else in his department to do so. The ruse worked, however, and "good old _____" *did* get active. Curriculum reforms in his department began within the year.

This same headmaster was equally effective in dealing with another problem endemic to prep schools: salary raises based on the "squeakiness of the wheel." One of my older colleagues was well known for his teaching skills and devotion to his work and students. But he also was notorious for his lack of assertiveness and therefore received no meaningful annual salary increases for years. Newly hired teachers, fresh out of college, might make more than him. The injustice of this was noted by the headmaster in question soon after he arrived on campus. He quite correctly viewed the matter as an ethical issue. Besides providing a sub-stantive raise, he also arranged for this teacher to receive a Donner Foundation grant to help reimburse him for the past injustice.

For years prep schools were able to get away with incredibly low faculty salaries, and my faculty respondents suggest that many still do. This is accomplished by various means. For one, faculty salaries often are kept secret to a degree unheard of at most other institutions. Even *ranges* of salaries that might be expected after a specified number of years of service are kept secret if, indeed, such ranges exist at all. Using an anonymous questionnaire, a faculty committee at one school tried to obtain information regarding salaries in an attempt to correct inequities. In a meeting with the headmaster, the committee was informed that variations in salary compositions would make it difficult if not impossible to determine anything valid from the responses. As a substitute, in a memo from the faculty representatives on the committee to the faculty, the headmaster announced that he would review the philosophical basis of the salary system. His review was presented orally at the end of a faculty meeting, allowing no time for discussion. One committee member told me that the headmaster had responded to their activities as if they were an attack on his personal integrity and that the committee itself was made to feel as if they were disloyal troublemakers.

I have seen this sort of response from more than one headmaster. It reflects the nature of the position, the psyche of the individuals who elect to occupy it, and the consolidation of power it represents. A faculty member's status within the prep school community often is a reflection of how the headmaster views him or her. Thus a feeling of insecurity develops that profoundly discourages openness and further investigations into "controversial" areas. Such a system allows for many abuses, including salary inequities. One female reviewer of an early version of this chapter, a prep school faculty member, commented:

> Right on! I sense a good deal of sexism in salary levels as well. I and many female friends were consistently paid less at [her school] than our male counterparts.

There has always been in prep schools a mind-set that it was a privilege to teach at such-and-such a school and that complaining was simply being whiny. Faculty members themselves are gulled by this ploy, making such self-serving comments as, "I can't believe they pay me for this job." Such remarks are sure-fire candidates for quotation in the alumni news.

I do not intend to denigrate the truly excellent prep school teachers who have worked for a pittance over the years. Rather, I merely point out that such heroic efforts should not be mutually exclusive with decent wages. The idea that teachers are happy to work for a pittance often is presented to alumni, whose contributions are an important part of a prep school's financial health. One old Mount Hermon graduate, when asked to donate for building renovation and faculty salaries, allegedly snorted, "Hmpfh! In my day, Mr. Cutler lectured to us in an unheated classroom with one bare light bulb over our heads and he was happy just to get his food and a roof over his head!" The nature of the comment is significant. In prep schools suffering equates to virtue, educational or otherwise. Gather any ten prep school teachers together and there will be at least one or two who will fill the air with comments about how many papers they graded last night, how many student personal problems they solved, and so forth. The stories are probably true, but they are the self-inflicted lashes of a penitent. They paint a self-portrait of sacrifice and devotion. Concerning this equating of suffering with educational virtue, departing Phillips Exeter Academy principal Kendra Stearns O'Donnell spoke in an interview of her impressions of the school community when she first arrived to take over the reins in 1987:

> Exeter seemed to me to be unduly uptight, given the people who were here. I mean, these were people who I thought were very interesting, very committed, fundamentally very lively people. I found myself asking, why this air of oppression hanging about so many adults and so many students? What is this all about . . . it seemed to be tied into the institution itself. In one opening Assembly, I talked about it as "the beast in the bricks." You couldn't point your finger at any particular source. Nobody seemed to own this force that was so oppressing us and clearly was creating a lot of the culture, expectations of a certain reserve, a certain grim formality, expectations of a kind of necessary suffering, all of which were presented as conditions essential for learning. This just struck me as — well — certainly something to be questioned! And it was all attached to something that no one could really name, that appeared to be in the bricks and in the place, not in the hearts and mind of the people. (*Exeter: The Bulletin of Phillips Exeter Academy,* 1997, p. 9)

One feature of prep schools is how they become both home and family to those who teach in them. Indeed, in my own experience it was not unusual to find faculty or staff members who had attended the school for which they were now working. In the two cases I can immediately recall, the time away from the prep school was only the four years it took to gain the bachelor's degree. The individuals I recall were student leaders while at their schools or had at least achieved some measure of success not matched in college. Like the old grad who, during an alumni weekend, returns to the stadium where he scored the winning touchdown against an archrival, they seemed to wish to recapture the warmth and feelings of self-worth provided in those earlier years. For some, such returns are successful; for others, they are not. As for any child who goes away to college and returns home as an adult, things are never the same. Reality replaces nostalgia, and a person may move from prep school to prep school in search of an elusive ideal that, almost certainly, never existed.

Equally interesting are the children of prep school faculty or staff who return, either to the same prep school or a similar one, to teach or work in some capacity. The Fall 1986 issue of *The Archon*, Governor Dummer Academy's magazine, notes one case in which three children of a prep school teacher became prep school teachers themselves. This "incestuous" character of prep schools is a phenomenon that is common knowledge to all prep school teachers. Its widespread existence has much to say about the way in which the ambiance of prep school life touches deeply those who have spent their lives in them. In my experience, among those returning "children of the schools," one often finds the best contributors to campus life, possibly because they believe deeply in the schools and know their inner workings well.

Administratively, prep schools share one other feature with colleges and universities: Without the nonfaculty and administrative personnel (infirmary nurses, secretaries, maintenance engineers, custodians), they would soon cease to function. Unfortunately, also shared is a tendency to devalue such personnel by referring to them as "nonprofessionals" or "the staff." Despite the equal importance of both faculty and staff to the operation of the school, prep school employees often are segregated by status (which often mirrors economic class), even in the school directories. Not surprisingly, such segregation carries over into the daily routine. For example, at lunch I rarely observed staff and faculty at the same table. It is unlikely that this distinction is missed by the students, for whom faculty members supposedly serve as role models. Certainly, such segregation merely reflects the tendency of our society to devalue certain occupations while exaggerating the importance of others. Yet, by allowing it to continue, prep schools contradict their claims to leadership in the realm of social ethics and justice. My interviews with prep school personnel suggest that, if the schools are looking for oppressed people to help, their own backyards would be a good place to start. Their "nonprofessional" staff are among the first to be exploited financially and the last to be recognized for exceptional merit.

It is not just a matter of pay. Rather, staff believe they are viewed by the faculty as a lower class of individuals; and surely it is their perceptions, rather than ours, that count here. Some schools make feeble attempts at equality, but these are usually in the form of receptions at the headmaster's house or annual community banquets. Twice at such events I saw new, single, male faculty members approach women staff members, only to lose interest immediately on learning that they were secretaries, not faculty colleagues. My experience at four very different schools has convinced me that, with the possible exceptions of prestigious and potentially influential staff positions (for example, the school head's secretary), class distinctions and academic snobbery are common themes on many prep school campuses.

A few schools are making at least some efforts toward improvement. For example, some campus directories no longer list faculty and staff separately. Such symbolic acts are very important. Yet rare, indeed, is the staff person who, privately at least, will not maintain there is still a very long way to go. One incident perhaps encapsulates it all. A secretary, working overtime at the request of the school and with her younger sister in her care,

asked the school librarian if the sister could use the school library
to work on a paper assigned for homework by her public school.
The librarian's curt refusal: The library is "only for the use of the
students and faculty."

Ironically, faculty (and most certainly students) recognize that
if one really wants to know what is going on in a prep school, it
is the "nonprofessionals" who know. Such persons were often
identified by the students in my survey as being the most trustworthy of confidants. One strong impression I received from
reading and listening to student comments is that, when it came
to mature attitudes about personal problems, the wrong people
had the keys. For example, noting that, as one put it, "most teachers were not open to having relaxed and open discussions about
sex," many students appeared to view the *faculty*, rather than
themselves, as the ones with problems. One male student wrote:

> Our school had house counselors who were not regular
> members of the faculty. Some were really uptight about sex,
> even pulling fire alarms in the middle of parietals. But on the
> whole they were better than the faculty, who were real ass-
> holes for the most part.

A woman graduate of one of the schools wrote:

> The [school] faculty was not understanding or helpful in
> matters of sex. It was treated like a "sin," and people who
> were caught were thrown out. The infirmary was a good
> place for students because they kept total confidentiality
> from the faculty, and the staff there could be trusted to deal
> maturely with the students.

Unless one has been involved in prep schools for a number of
years, it is difficult to imagine what a shock it would be to most
school faculty to learn that students view members of the staff to
be more trustworthy and mature than the faculty. Yet, though it
pains me to admit it, I think this perception, more often than not,
is correct. In responding to the faculty-versus-staff maturity issue
and in defense of the faculty, one prep school teacher reviewer of
the manuscript of this book inadvertently put her finger on what

may well be the crux of the problem — the subverting of individual values to those of the school — when she wrote: "Faculty are expected to enforce school rules. . . no matter what our own personal values are, whereas staff are usually not expected to."

Headmaster Rae actually suggests a positive role for faculty immaturity:

> To achieve the ideal requires maturity and self-discipline on the part of the teachers. How many teachers are mature? I sometimes wonder. The profession seems to attract more than its share of angular and quirky personalities. Where would our memories of childhood be without them? Could it be that children need to be taught by some nut cases, that they wouldn't cope with a teaching force of normal, balanced adults, just as it would be difficult for children to cope with perfect parents? Perhaps the children need to encounter some inadequate personalities in the classroom in order to give them confidence that adulthood is not so difficult to achieve, after all. (1987, p. 149)

Rae is probably correct concerning the harmlessness of a few faculty "nut cases." However, I recall early in my teaching career encountering one that was far from positive for me. A middle-aged history teacher took an inordinate amount of interest in me. He would confront me on campus to declare his love, and I found myself skipping meals (which we all ate together) and sneaking around campus in order to avoid him (the days of assertiveness for women were still far in the future). The situation was further complicated by an architectural oddity that made it impossible for me to reach my classroom without walking through his, with the result that he would interrupt his lectures to tell his students of his adoration. I actually found myself climbing in the window of my classroom to avoid contact! I was lucky in having a supportive and sympathetic headmaster, and the situation was finally resolved by this man leaving the school for another teaching position. Although most of the faculty recognized this person as most definitely an "odd duck" and quite likely harmless, I recall that at times I felt so uncomfortable in his presence that the emotion approached genuine fear.

One behavior pattern widely recognized in some prep school faculty by both students and faculty colleagues is the person imbued with a "gotta-catch-'em-at-it" mentality. Such persons spend inordinate amounts of time sneaking along dormitory corridors, library stacks, or campus woods looking for rule breakers. They seem to gain an inordinate sense of satisfaction if they are successful and a sense of frustration if not. Such neurotic behavior is soon spotted by the students, who, of course, take a double delight in baiting these faculty. Unfortunately, many prep schools openly encourage this sort of faculty behavior, at times reinforcing it with promotions into positions of power. In terms of student attitudes toward the school, such practices backfire badly. As one student put it:

> Defiance is a big part of prep school because discipline is such a big part of prep school . . . we felt we had to beat the system that had screwed us over so many times.

This student, who specifically recognized the paranoia involved, wrote of his graduation day:

> We popped open our champagne and drank for the first time out in the open. We toasted boldly those teachers who, prior to graduation, would have loved to have caught us drinking so they could have us kicked out. Now all they could do was glare! We were loving every minute of it. After the reception we raced each other off campus as a testimony to how much we couldn't stand the place. . . . Now, I wonder. Was it some great oppressive institution? In reality, it was just a prep school.

CHAPTER 4

Religion and Values

"The practical value of such a close connection between Chapel and Schoolhouse is obvious, but it has also a symbolic value. Life in the school is never to be far removed from those values and attitudes which are shaped by life in the Chapel. The two are structurally and organically connected and cannot be separated without damage to both. So also the learning and the daily living of St. George's and its religious life and aims are part and parcel of the same educational process."

— Undated pamphlet from St. George's School Chapel

The founding of the elite prep schools included a great deal of religious tradition. Thus it is not surprising, as Cookson and Persell (1985) point out, that these schools placed moral character first and intellectual qualities last when they chose headmasters. The headmaster was supposed to be a moral role model for both students and faculty. Such a sanctimonious attitude is far less common today, and it would come as a shock to the school founders to learn that the students in my sample regarded school chapels as one of the safest places for "making out."

This religious tradition has had a great effect on the prep schools' self-images. Most schools' founders closely linked higher education with mainstream Protestant Christianity, and some forms of Protestantism were considered more socially acceptable than others. Nor was this ranking of denominations limited to prep schools. For example, biographer Ted Morgan notes that

Franklin Delano Roosevelt's father "made the move from the Dutch Reformed to the more socially correct Episcopalian faith" (1985, p. 32). This move from an evangelical to a more orthodox and socially acceptable form of Protestant Christianity has at least a symbolic significance in viewing New England college preparatory schools historically in terms of their prestige.

Until recently, if one were to read articles or books about the elite, prestigious New England college preparatory schools, Northfield Mount Hermon was rarely included. On first glance, it is difficult to see why this should be the case. The Northfield Mount Hermon campus, described as being almost one-third the size of Manhattan, dwarfs those of most other schools and colleges; and its physical facilities, worth approximately twice those of Choate-Rosemary Hall, are superb. More important, the caliber of the faculty and student body is assuredly as good as those of the others.

In truth, the reasons for Northfield Mount Hermon being overlooked are almost certainly historical and of considerable significance to an understanding of the prep school self-image. Just as we get in the habit of listing Harvard, Yale, and Princeton when referring to outstanding colleges, despite the fact that we all know of other colleges and universities of comparable academic status, so, too, is this the case with prep schools. Though secular now, Harvard, Yale, and Princeton were founded with a white, male, and Christian viewpoint. Whether stated explicitly or not, so also were such schools as Andover, Exeter, Deerfield, and Groton. However, the version of Christianity such schools represented was generally considered to be mainline and respectable and one that provided all the comforts of that religion with none of the social stigmas connected to fundamentalist evangelical Protestantism (in those days, Roman Catholicism was considered too far beyond the social and intellectual pale to be taken seriously). Then, much as today, evangelical Protestantism was associated with the uneducated lower classes and thus considered far removed from the intellectual and business interests of most of the prestigious schools' founders.

It was just such an association — evangelistic, fundamentalist Protestantism — that characterized the beginning of The Northfield School for Girls (1879) and Mount Hermon School for Boys (1881), now the coeducational Northfield Mount Hermon. Their founder, a man who himself never went beyond the seventh grade, was Dwight L. Moody (1837–1899), whose name graces the strongly fundamentalist Moody Bible Institute in Chicago. Moody is a difficult man to characterize, and it is not essential to the point to do so here. It perhaps suffices merely to state that he was somewhat a 19th century counterpart to Billy Graham. In truth, such a comparison may be somewhat unfair to Moody, who spent much of his time working in the slums of Chicago. Nor was Moody's evangelism tainted with the racism that has tended to characterize its counterpart in other regions of the country, especially the South. As then Northfield Mount Hermon school head Jacqueline Smethurst noted in the fall 1996 issue of the school's magazine, *The News*, the four student speakers at the first Mount Hermon graduation were African American, Chinese, Choctaw, and white. Finally, it is worth noting that the Northfield School for Girls was founded by Moody at a time when many, if not most, Christian denominations were politically active in opposing education for females, suggesting that Moody had a progressive, rather than reactionary, view of the world.

Many of Mount Hermon School's early students were from urban slums. Quartered in a farmhouse, the "boys," many of them actually in their 20s, became exposed to a tough regimen of studies and the physical labor that characterized a 19th century farm — which, in fact, is precisely what Mount Hermon was. The student work program was more than an economic necessity for the school's survival, for Moody was a strong believer in the dignity of so-called menial labor. A work program of 10 hours per week per student, regardless of means, still characterized the Northfield Mount Hermon program when I taught there.

Interestingly, the Loomis Institute (the Loomis Chaffee School) founded with a far more secular philosophy than was Northfield Mount Hermon, also had a shared-by-all chores program. Though today some schools (for example, Kent) do have a student work program, one of the sort that D.L. Moody established would not have gone over at most of those prep schools whose students were then almost entirely from the wealthy elite.

It took Mount Hermon a long time to emerge from the intellectually stultifying effects of its fundamentalist background. As late as the early 1950s, the teaching of evolution in biology classes was forbidden and the faculty had to sneak to play cards. The move away from the school's early puritanical philosophy was begun in the 1930s by a headmaster who introduced such radical measures as allowing afternoon tea dances at Mount Hermon with the girls from Northfield and even brought to campus an Arthur Murray dance instructor to teach the students how to dance. For these and other such liberalizing measures, he was promptly murdered.*

Almost certainly, the omission of Northfield Mount Hermon from lists of the academically and socially prestigious New England college preparatory schools is related historically to its religious background. To have compared an Exeter or Andover to Mount Hermon as these schools were, say, in the 1920s, would be similar to today comparing Harvard University to Wheaton College (Illinois), Jerry Falwell's Liberty Baptist, or the Bob Jones University in Greenville, South Carolina. In prep schools, as in good colleges and universities, religious dogmatism, both Protestant and Catholic, has been and still is considered an antithesis to achieving widely recognized academic excellence in the liberal arts sense of the term.

The evangelistic fundamentalism that marked its beginning may have prevented Northfield Mount Hermon from being recognized as being on a par with the more socially and intellectu-

---

*Headmaster Elliot Speer was killed by a shotgun blast through the window of his study in the headmaster's house on the Mount Hermon campus. The murder is still listed as one of the great unsolved crimes of the 20th century. Although the finger of suspicion pointed strongly to a fundamentalist school administrator who bitterly resented Speer's modernization efforts, failure to find the murder weapon made a conviction impossible.

ally acceptable mainline religious background of such elite schools as Deerfield or Groton. Were the Northfield Mount Hermon school of today to be as its founder might have wished, it would be as much an anomaly among New England prep schools as would Bob Jones University in the Ivy League. However, it is equally clear that Northfield Mount Hermon is one of the best college preparatory schools in the country and may even be superior, academically, to some of the better-known ones. Yet for financial reasons, Northfield Mount Hermon, like Janus, must present two faces; one for the older alumni who remember the school when it was still in the D.L. Moody image and another for those who realize the school must remain academically competitive. This mixed image became most evident to me when my husband and I were invited back to the school for an alumni reunion (We had served as advisers to the Mount Hermon Class of 1961). We were greeted at the registration site by a group around a table inviting us to "sign up for Jesus." Yet the weekend's program was clearly of a more academic bent, including an excellent Charles Darwin exhibit done by a female biology teacher on the Northfield Mount Hermon faculty.

My former Mount Hermon faculty colleague William R. Compton has written an article attempting to bridge the gap between Moody's evangelism and Northfield Mount Hermon's current modern educational outlook. Compton notes correctly that the Moody Bible Institute in Chicago was (and is) entirely fundamentalist in its outlook, but he suggests that its namesake was far more tolerant of diverse views, even refusing to condemn outright a "modernist" friend who had embraced evolution. An excellent article, it still falls far short of being convincing concerning how Moody would view his school today. The conflicts that dragged Northfield Mount Hermon into the modern intellectual world, as Compton himself notes, "seem nowadays almost as far off in time as Mr. Moody himself" (1988, pp. 14-16).

Writing in the Spring 1994 issue of *The News*, James Dunaway, Northfield Mount Hermon's academic dean and teacher in the religious studies department, said that Mr. Moody's school is "not a religious school," but teaches about humankind's various religious mythologies because of the school's recognition that "anyone who is ignorant of the manifold ways in which religious traditions have affected human history and experience will be unable to interpret world events, not to mention the events in their own lives."

The better-known New England prep schools do not have such a wide gap between their religious backgrounds and their current academic excellence and respectability. One reason is that their founders viewed higher education, linked closely with Protestant Christianity, as a means to enhance this respectability and to provide an entry into the world of financial success. Only the influx of Jewish and Roman Catholic students over the past two or three decades has forced a broader view. Phillips Andover, for example, now has a Jesuit chaplain for Roman Catholic students and a Rabbi for Jewish students. For most of their history, however, the schools had a male chaplain for all students, and he was always Christian, always Protestant. Nor has the nostalgia for those days disappeared; I recently read a chapel speech by a prep school teacher of ten years who stated that, despite certain of his school's faults, "at least it was Christian."

Most New England college preparatory schools report that they emphasize religion in the formulation of student values. Yet, Cookson and Persell report that only 4% of prep school students remember their exposure to religion at their schools 10 years after graduation and none remember it as the most valuable aspect of their boarding school experience. My own research also suggests that religious values have little effect on students. For example, in response to the true-false question, "I believe that God is interested in my sexual behavior," the vast majority of both prep school students and college-bound public school students marked "false." Perhaps more interesting is that almost 80% of both male and female prep school students in my sample, for whom religion courses are offered or required, checked "false" to the above question, while slightly more than 70% of their public school counterparts did so. In addition, a question asking respondents to rate themselves on a scale of 1 to 10 as either "very religious" or "not religious at all" revealed that both prep school males and females rated themselves as less religious than did their public school counterparts.

While religion may not score highly in surveys of students, it is certain that these schools do attempt to teach values. In a letter to parents and students, one headmaster wrote:

> moral education — the formation of good character and habits of right conduct — is the joint responsibility of the family and the school. . . . Although much learning about values takes place in academic work, and not only in philosophy and religion courses, it is the whole way of life of the school which serves us, teacher and student alike, as a workshop in which to sharpen our definitions of acceptable and unacceptable behavior.

Certainly there is much here with which one can agree. While there may still be a few diehards around, the idea that one can teach anything, even nuclear physics, without making at least one or two value statements is now passé. If one teaches nuclear physics, for example, and includes a discussion of the weaponry the field has made possible, value judgments *pro* or *con* are necessarily involved, even if not verbalized in the classroom. To teach nuclear physics and ignore the issue is equally a value statement. When, in the school prayer issue, the religious right states that disallowing prayer in public schools is, in itself, a value statement, they are absolutely right. It was precisely such a value judgment that led to the doctrine of the separation of church and state and Thomas Jefferson's Statute of Religious Freedom. This value judgment was a vital component of a mechanism designed to correct the cruel abuses of religious freedom that characterized both the Western Europe from which the Pilgrims fled (abuses they then promptly introduced into New England) and much of Colonial America as well.

However, the more critical issue here is not whether values are or are not to be a part of a secondary student's education. For good or for bad, they are. The essential point is: *Whose* values? In commenting on the teaching of morals, Sizer comments:

> private school people, particularly those in church schools, tend to be more aggressive about the goal, though for many of them the line between religious doctrine is seriously blurred, begging clarification. (1984, p. 122)

And later,

> Resurgent Fundamentalist Christianity serves to remind educators of how intrusive religious matter is in all schools, however pugnaciously secular they may proclaim themselves. The neat legalisms about Jefferson's putative wall between Church and State find no place for reality, save at the extremes. (p. 129)

Few familiar with secondary school education, public *or* private, would argue with the first quoted statement. It is not clear from the second statement, however, whether Sizer is suggesting that, because of the "intrusive" nature of religion into education, one must be ever more vigilant to ensure that the constitutional guarantee of the separation of church and state be preserved or that we must give up on the idea that it can ever be kept that way. His comment that in private schools, especially, the line is "seriously blurred" would support the first of these interpretations. Yet, elsewhere, Sizer appears to surrender to the inevitability of a connection between a teacher's ethics and religion when he writes:

> The most accepted American secular ethic is a direct extension of Judeo-Christian teaching, and cannot be detached from it, however hard the constitutional lawyers may labor. (p. 129)

Yet, this "direct extension" comment is both true and not true. No less of an apologist for Christianity than C. S. Lewis pointed out long ago that virtually none of the tenets in the Ten Commandments or the Sermon on the Mount are original with either Judaism or Christianity, but rather owe their origins to other, much older religious traditions. What can be said is that Judaism and Christianity, as much as any other religiously based philosphy, have served to focus these ethical principles into a coherent whole. However, to attempt to convince students that these ethical principles are unique to Judaism or Christianity is to twist history to fit our values. Worse, it fosters a chauvinistic view of other religions with somewhat differing interpretations and values. So doing is not education, it is indoctrination.

In this same context of education versus indoctrination and the religious bigotry that is often the result of the latter, another incident is of particular interest here. The Spring 1986 Northfield Mount Hermon alumni magazine, *The News*, carried a letter from an early alumna expressing her opinion that "the clear Christian focus of D.L. Moody appears to be watered down." Even more explicit, however, was another letter's reference to the previous issue's cover illustration of Northfield Mount Hermon dance students performing an Indian dance:

> This message is to protest the cover photo on the Winter 1986 issue of *The News*. Should a Christian school celebrate a pagan Hindu festival? I am outraged and angry! Oh, how far we have strayed from our Lord's ideals and our founder D. L. Moody's aspirations for the School.

Equally telling was the editor's response:

> The most recent cover of *The News* has generated many positive and negative reactions. It should be noted that, although the students are depicted acting out a Hindu myth, the dance they performed (from which the idea for the photograph was spawned) was an original performance conceived and expertly choreographed by Patricia Smith, NMH's performing dance instructor.

Note how the wording carefully distances the Northfield Mount Hermon dance students and the school from the "Hindu myth." Instead, the students are merely "acting out" an intellectual conception of their instructor. The depth and meaning of a religious rite sacred to millions of human beings is thereby surgically removed so as to placate, rather than confront, the writer's religious bigotry. How refreshing it would have been to have read: "We see no more reason to be offended by Northfield Mount Hermon students performing a dance in honor of a Hindu myth than should graduates of a school in India be offended at seeing students carrying out a dance in honor of a Christian myth." Alas, to do so would bring screams of outrage from old alumni, to whom "myth" is what those Hindu and other pagans believe; the Truth is what *we* believe. One might guess that the sound of those alumni purses snapping shut would be positively deafening.

Almost all of the leading New England prep schools and colleges were strongly religious at their founding. While some may not have had Northfield Mount Hermon's four years of required Bible classes, they certainly revealed an enthusiasm for Christianity through organized prayer, compulsory chapel attendance, faculty-led religious discussions, and so forth. Nor is this unknown today. A Groton catalogue, for example, restates its founder Reverend Endicott Peabody's intent "that religion not only be an important part of the official life of the Groton School, but also make a claim on the entirety of life," and as far as I know, except for Saturdays, Groton still has a required daily chapel. So, too, does Kent school. Lateness to chapel can result, as one disgruntled Kent student put it, in being "stung four hours." I must stress again, however, the religious viewpoint of such schools was (and to a large extent still is) mainline, reflecting an upper-class, socially acceptable version of Christianity.

While such schools may have espoused liberal forms of Christianity, they also shared with their fundamentalist brethren a marked antipathy, if not outright hostility, to those whose religious views differed from theirs, notably Jews and Roman Catholics. At the time I joined the Mount Hermon faculty, I was the first Roman Catholic allowed to teach there. Only one Jew had ever been on the faculty. In the latter case several colleagues of this person frankly admitted that his life at the school had been made miserable, and he soon left to join the faculty of another prep school with weaker ideological roots. However, I experienced little or no difficulty, possibly because my non-Catholic husband had preceded me on the faculty or simply because the school was that much further removed in time from its evangelical base. Interestingly, when we left Mount Hermon for a year so that my husband could return to graduate school and were then invited to return, the new headmaster, who had been hired while we were away, felt it necessary to check my religious views to ensure that they were acceptable to the community as he viewed it from his Presbyterian minister's perspective.

Since many of today's young faculty members understandably resent their school's attempts to control their lives or, in some cases, to make conformity of their personal views or lifestyles with the philosophy of the school a condition for employment, I have often wondered why I was so accepting of, rather than angry at, having my religious views questioned by the headmaster. There are several possible reasons, of course. For one, Roman Catholics in the 1950s and earlier were so accustomed to such discrimination that, like many other groups so victimized, we often accepted it as inevitable. Yet, in truth, much of the blame for this discrimination against Roman Catholics must be laid at the door of the church that was supposed to be sustaining them. Those of us who attended parochial schools were often poorly educated. Furthermore, in those pre-Vatican II days, one had to get permission from a parish priest in order to attend a Protestant church, even for a wedding or funeral! As for "those perfidious Jews," forget it! We were informed in parochial school that we belonged to the "one true Church." From his viewpoint as a Presbyterian minister, the headmaster's concern was a quite legitimate one, and I later came to respect him as much as any person for whom I have worked.

There are encouraging signs that prep schools are beginning to recognize that not all of the world's peoples view matters through Judeo-Christian eyes. Interestingly, one of the most encouraging signs comes from Northfield Mount Hermon. *The News* editor who responded so meekly to the angry alumna concerning the "pagan Hindu myth" would have done well to have read his own administration's views. In the Spring 1986 issue of *The News*, then headmaster Richard P. Unsworth (a Protestant minister and graduate of the school) responded to the question, "By the way you speak about the 'spiritual,' do you mean organized religion? Does Northfield-Mount Hermon have an official church affiliation?" He wrote:

> No, we're specifically non-denominational. There are organized church activities for the major faiths each week on campus, but attendance is invited, not required. Our founder, D.L. Moody, was a nineteenth century Protestant evangelist with an international reputation. One of our main legacies at the School is an awareness of the importance of studying religion and how it affects the whole of the human condition. Study of the Bible is included because it is the portable homeland of Western civilization. But we also study the Koran, and the writings of Buddha, Mohammed, Nietzsche, Gandhi and Socrates among others. I think you see what I mean. Our emphasis recognizes the importance of structured religion, but it does not exclude other things. My training here, and later in divinity school, taught me that Jesus' ministry did not focus in the synagogues. Where did he do his "spiritual cultivation"? In the vineyards, by a well, on a street corner. It was done in relation to the whole of life — not secreted away somewhere for the benefit of a righteous few.

Such an ecumenical view would have been impossible during the early years of most prep schools. Its educational importance can hardly be overestimated in a world in which we must deal both socially and politically with people whose religious beliefs encompass different views of reality.

Probably most contemporary prep school heads would find themselves in essential agreement with Unsworth's views. Unfortunately, their schools tend to treat other religious viewpoints as inferior in comparison to Judaism and, especially, Christianity. Such deception is not lost on faculty or students. As one respondent put it:

> One thing I *really* noticed — they tried to project the image of being liberal and open minded, but it really wasn't there.

Another, though acknowledging that there *were* efforts to present other viewpoints, still noted that "the school didn't really leave it up to us, but wanted us to come to the 'right' decision."

Obviously, both these students (and many others) felt they were being conned and expressed anger at being thus used. What might have been a valuable educational experience became, instead, fertile ground for unproductive cynicism.

This is not to suggest that students should be taught that all value systems are of equal worth. However, we must make our criteria for holding one system of values better than another crystal clear. Whenever we discuss values, our premises are themselves based on value judgments. For example, in a letter to parents and students, one headmaster asks, "How do you understand the virtues that are necessary for the good life: honesty, compassion for others, self-restraint, and responsibility for one's actions?" Note that no one can answer this question without accepting its basic premises. Yet this premise is based on value judgments concerning what constitutes "the good life." We can take the "virtue" of "self-restraint" as an example. It is not an uncommon one to find being stressed at prep schools. Another headmaster writes in his school's catalogue about "teaching how to discriminate between a good life and a bad life" and implies that acquiring "habits of self-control" is an essential step in doing so. However, the "self-restraints" that schools reinforce, or punish when not followed, are often very much time- and culture-bound. In the Winter 1987 issue of her school's magazine, the *Bulletin of Miss Porter's School*, former Miss Porter's School head Rachel Belash writes:

> I think back to what was expected of girls growing up when I did and I recall, only too acutely, that before all else we were taught to seek approval. The adults around us, kind and humane as they were, had tremendous power over us — the power to disapprove. There were many things that drew disapproval, but they could be categorized as "unladylike," "too Tomboyish," "too daring," "aggressive," "pushy," "bossy". . . in a word, "unfeminine." And the dreaded result

of losing approval? Someone might not like us. This was terrible, probably because it implied that if we were unlikable, next we would be unmarriageable, indeed an unspeakable fate. So we courted approval, we were good girls, we said and did what people expected, we were charming nonpersons.

As Belash suggests, self-restraint or self-control are supposedly laudatory characteristics that many persons, especially women, have had thoroughly drilled into them, and certainly her references to the "tremendous power" schools can wield in controlling behavior is a point well taken. One has only to pick up any of dozens of autobiographies or articles to read that, in the viewpoint of their authors, they did not achieve "the good life" until they critically reexamined the historical and political roots of the rules and "self-restraints" imposed on them by society. By so doing, such individuals have found the educational experience to be a liberalizing one. Some decided that, for them, this restraint was beneficial. For others, it was oppressive. Whatever the outcome, each adjusted their lives accordingly. The point is that, only by allowing students to see the underlying premises of the value systems to which they are exposed, rather than simply the value systems themselves, can we honestly maintain that we have exposed them to the true meaning of a liberal education. In the case of Judaism and Christianity, for example, female students especially should be made aware of their historical patriarchal bias. The degree to which the "self-restraint" and "self-control" theme has been used in these religions throughout history to control women's behavior very much reflects a male view of the way things ought to be.

There also is a genuine danger in confusing ethical values or actions with religious beliefs to the extent of making the former a subset of the latter. By so doing, one excludes a long list of distinguished religious doubters. An example is humanist Corliss Lamont, a 1920 Phillips Exeter Academy graduate, who was honored by that school in 1987 with its prestigious John Phillips award. Such persons have had much to say about ethical values and actions that are well worth our attention and that of our students. Yet even today one often finds prep schools linking values or morals exclusively to Judeo-Christian roots, with a strong emphasis on the latter.*

Theodore Sizer, himself a former headmaster (Phillips Academy, Andover), makes an explicit connection between ethics and religion:

> Decency in the American tradition (obviously the creation more of our Judeo-Christian than our republican tradition) comprises fairness, generosity, and tolerance. (1984, p. 121)

Later, still in the context of a Judeo-Christian view, he writes:

> Individualism, compassion, the sense of obligation for service to one's community, and belief in literacy all have, surprising as it might seem to some, religious roots. (1984, p. 127)

So they do. Yet none of these attributes are exclusive to Jewish or Christian teachings, nor are they necessarily best exemplified by them. "The Golden Rule" is not exclusively a Christian precept. It appears in Egyptian myth, Confucianism, Buddhism, and Islamic teachings, as well as in the writings of the Hebrew Bible (Old Testament) prophets. Beyond that, we must be honest with our students and admit that at almost any point in history one can find large segments of Christian thought and action that not only failed to encourage individualism but, with an almost unimaginable cruelty, tried to suppress it. As for "literacy," for most of its history the Church spent far more time trying to keep it within the ranks of its clergy than it did in trying to spread it among the laity. The Protestant Reformation marked a beginning, to be sure. Yet by no means even then was the idea of a literate laity welcomed by the clergy. When it was, the learning was for more of an indoc-

---

*The reason given for studying the Old Testament at one school in which I taught was that Judaism was the soil from which the seed of Christianity sprouted. Such an analogy denigrates the former into a mere culture medium, without aesthetic value except for the organism it enabled to grow.

trination into the Christian view of the world than an education in the true liberal arts sense.

I have devoted space to religion in this discussion of prep schools because it is so much a part of their historical development and therefore crucial to the value-based attitudes about sex and sexuality perceived by the students and faculty of the schools in my sample. From what my student and faculty sample populations tell me, their schools convey a negative attitude toward sex that is derived from their Christianity, which anthropologist Nigel Davies (1984) called the most "sex-negative" of all religions. The image of her school conveyed by one student respondent was reflected, sadly, in the comments of many others from every school on my list:

> The headmistress was an ex-nun. One day she saw graffiti on walls and really freaked out. She felt students' minds must be in the gutters to do such things. If a female student became pregnant, she would be sent home. If an unmarried female faculty member became pregnant, she would be fired *immediately*. If faculty members of the opposite sex were living together, the school would pretend they were married and they would have to move off campus.

If Sizer is correct that "students learn much from the way a school is run" (1984, p. 120), what this student learned from her school is appalling indeed. One could hardly find a worse example of fairness, compassion, or respect for individualism — precisely those qualities Sizer associates with the Judeo-Christian tradition — to say nothing of a better example of institutional hypocrisy. Far more often than I would have believed, this perception of their schools by both students and faculty came across loud and clear.

Sizer is devastating in the case he makes against mandatory or even voluntary prayer in public schools, pointing out that it will inevitably serve only to trivialize religion. However, he then goes on to state:

> Clearly, schools are expected by most Americans to stand
> for certain values and to inculcate those in their students.
> Most of these values have religious roots, if not strict theo-
> logical identification today. Educators who pretend that
> these are purely secular values are whistling in the dark.
> (p. 129)

No one denies that most values have religious roots. However,
does making a value a religious one make the adherence to that
value any more likely? There is a long history of prep schools
believing this to be the case. The Governor Dummer School 1987
Catalog notes that the school was founded in 1743 "for the promotion of piety and virtue," and its founders seriously believed
that one followed the other. Phillips Academy, Andover and
Phillips Academy, Exeter had similar statements concerning their
founding. Even today, one finds this viewpoint alive and well. An
advertisement for St. Anne's-Belfield School (located in Charlottesville, Virginia) claims that the school's "weekly chapel and
community service promote moral development and a concern
for others."* In the school sexual assault incident I cited in the introduction, the fact that all students "are obliged to attend school
and take religious instruction" is mentioned by the newspaper
account in a manner implying that this fact should have prevented
the incident. In a reaction to a rash of thefts at Kent (a common,
almost cyclical occurrence at prep schools), a letter to the editor
in the 15 November 1986 *Kent News* reads, "If Kent were an ideal
environment, its inhabitants would respect the fundamental
Christian foundations that the school was based upon," a statement that clearly associates Christianity with theft prevention. In
the Summer 1988 issue of *Kent Quarterly*, Kent headmaster
Father Richardson W. Schell (Kent, Class of 1969) quotes Professor James Q. Wilson to the effect that "religion has a significant effect in keeping young people out of trouble."

---

*I saw this advertisement for the school in the February/March 1993 issue of
Albemarle Magazine.

Intuitively one suspects that this religion = virtue equation does not hold true. Indeed, while researching this topic, I came upon one situation in which a religious viewpoint seemed to *block* sensitivity to an ethical issue. The Winter 1993 *Archon*, the bulletin of Governor Dummer Academy, carried an interview with an incoming president of its board of trustees. The article did not censor out the interviewee's occasional expletive use of "God" and "Jesus Christ," an omission that led two clergymen graduates of the school to write strong letters of protest that appeared in the following issue. However, both writers failed to note that Jesus' name was used in context of inadequate faculty compensation, clearly an ethical issue of exploitation.

A genuine trivializing of religion occurs when we insist on "theologizing," usually in a negative manner, perfectly natural processes. In no area has this occurred so widely as in the area of sexuality. As one of my faculty respondents suggested, when masturbation is described (as it is by the largest Christian denomination, Roman Catholicism) as a "seriously and intrinsically disordered act" (Sacred Congregation, 1975, p. 9) the silliness of such a teaching and its potential harm to mental health leads one to question the validity of other values held by this same religion that might deserve thoughtful attention.

The results of my study are hardly a glowing testimonial to the power of wrapping philosophical values in the clothing of Western religion. Yet at most, if not all, prep schools, religion and philosophy are unified into a single department as if they were one and the same. (There are historical reasons for this, of course, and the situation is found even at some colleges and universities.) Further, religion and ethics courses may be required, and one often finds individual faculty members from these departments actively involved in counseling, "values clarification" seminars, and courses in human sexuality. Yet, according to my study of prep school student sexual attitudes and behavior, the results are hardly a smashing triumph of religious good over evil. In the area of sexual attitudes and behavior, by their own stated criteria, there has obviously been a failure on the part of these schools to incul-

cate the desired values. To the degree that any school has implicated Judeo-Christian philosophy as being part of those values,
so, too, is that philosophy implicated in this failure.

As I noted earlier, there are encouraging signs that belief in a
direct cause-and-effect relationship between Western religious
beliefs and ethical actions is fading. An article in the Miss Porter's School *Bulletin* poses three questions of three former headmasters concerning ethics. Religion entered into their responses
only once, ironically centering on students refusing to obey the
school's then-church attendance requirement. The headmaster
involved confessed that he was in sympathy with the students but
continued the requirement because of the challenge to his authority. The requirement was later dropped ("Three Questions," 1987,
pp. 2-5).

There seems to be an increasing awareness on the part of the
schools that religious "truths" come in many forms and that they
are very much a product of the cultures in which they have
evolved. According to a former headmaster, St. Mark's School in
Southborough, Massachusetts, is unabashedly a Christian school.
Indeed, the school's promotional literature states so explicitly:
"Founded as an Episcopal school, St. Mark's remains firmly
grounded in the moral values of its Judaeo-Christian heritage."
Yet the statement goes on to stress that the school also is "committed to helping students develop *their own* faith, regardless of
individual heritage" (emphasis added). In keeping with the latter
pledge, besides those courses devoted to the Hebrew prophets
and Jesus (courses that also include the writings of Ghandi, Martin Luther King Jr., Thomas Merton, Dorothy Day, and Desmond
Tutu), are those such as "Eastern Religious Thought" and "History of Islam." There also was a course titled "Science and Religion," co-taught by persons from each department. Northfield
Mount Hermon, the school whose fundamentalist origins are
described in opening this chapter, now proudly proclaims the
presence on campus of faculty advisors and student groups supporting Roman Catholic, Hindu, Jewish, and Muslim faiths — all
begun by a Christian husband and wife chaplaincy team.

Equally encouraging is a beautifully written article in a Phillips Exeter Academy *Bulletin* by religion teacher Peter Vork-ink II, which notes that,

> the Religion Department curriculum has undergone considerable transformation in the past two decades. . . on one level we are trying to expose the student body to religious traditions from around the world, but on a deeper level we are trying to suggest that the many people and cultures of the world all think very differently and have very different sensibilities from what had been traditionally thought in the West. . . . These changes have less to do with the teaching of the basic knowledge of religion, either East or West, and more to do with . . . sharing very different thought-worlds [and] fundamentally different philosophical and cultural assumptions from what traditionally had been voiced. . . in the past. (1993, pp. 7-8)

In today's pluralistic world one could hardly imagine a better intellectual exposure for young people. For those of us in education, it is far better to admit that many forces — economic, educational, familial, political, psychological, *and* religious — help to form our values. Such an admission enables us to aid our students in understanding the subtle interactions of these forces and thereby to make decisions within the context of the intellectual freedom that a liberal arts education is meant to provide.

CHAPTER 5

Athletics and Values

"Our practices and policies are consistent with Preparatory School tradition, and are based on the belief that it is essential for our school to compete in athletics with the *'BEST SCHOOLS'*."
— Memo to a prep school faculty from
the chairman of the athletic department

"At most prep schools sport is about competition, and even more important, about winning."
— Cookson and Persell, *Preparing for Power,* p. 78

A 1980s Phillips Academy, Andover, bulletin relates the story of one Archie Bush, Class of 1866, who had returned to the school after the Civil War to complete his studies. While at Andover, he organized a baseball team. When he and some friends cut a geometry class to attend a game, all were expelled. Though this action was later rescinded by the board of trustees (too late for Archie, who had died in Europe while on his honeymoon), that the expulsion occurred at all is symbolic of the priorities then in effect at Andover concerning the relative importance of academics and athletics. While it might be an exaggeration to say that a contemporary Archie would be expelled for doing the reverse — cutting a baseball game to attend a geometry class — it is ironic to note that in recent years Andover has excused all students from a day of classes if they beat their great rival, Phillips Exeter, in football.

Such a turnaround is symbolic of a serious problem at many college preparatory schools — an increasing glorification of athletics at the expense of the academic program. In his annual review of the academic year 1985-86 in the *Loomis Chaffee School Bulletin*, headmaster John Ratté listed events that the graduating members of the class of 1986 would recall about their senior year. First on his list was athletics: "Members of the class of 1986 will remember being at school in the year in which both the boy's track team and girl's swimming team won the New Englands, even as the boy's and girl's lacrosse teams were undefeated in independent school play and won Founder's League titles." Next on the remembrance list were concerts and theatrical events, followed by discussions of South Africa, the Holocaust, Strategic Defense Initiative (which edged out "pool parties"), Senior Servant Day, and the various student publications.

St. George's School in Newport, Rhode Island, describes in a brochure how carved figures depicting football and baseball, representing the school's athletic program, appear in the passageway separating the chapel and the schoolhouse. The description is worded to imply that athletics at St. George's establishes a logical connection between the academic and the spiritual. Whether this actually is believed at St. George's, I cannot say. Yet one can pick up almost any prep school catalogue and read that sports "builds character." For example, in promotional literature sent to parents of prospective students in summer 1998, St. Mark's School in Southboro, Massachusetts, refers to "coach-inspired discipline" and maintains that their athletic program "helps build the character which is evident in its students' thoughts and actions every day, in every area of their lives." Kent School director of athletics Todd Marble is quoted by his headmaster as maintaining that "daily participation in athletic endeavors nurtures an internal discipline, mental and physical, which builds character both on and off the field of play." The headmaster goes on to state that "Good athletes and young people concerned about fitness do not, as a rule, abuse substances."

Perhaps at St. Mark's and Kent this is true. Yet the evidence is by no means overwhelming that it is the case elsewhere. Indeed, there exist considerable data supporting the contention that, instead, competitive sports tend to *reveal* character as well as to foster selfish motives and antisocial behavior. Most certainly there are many headlines about college and professional athletes that support this contention. Resolving the issue obviously lies well beyond the scope of this book, but those willing to at least consider this less popular alternative to the "sports builds character" hypothesis might wish to read *Lessons of the Locker Room: The Myth of School Sports*, by Andrew W. Miracle, Jr., professor of anthropology at Texas Christian University and C. Roger Rees, associate professor of physical education at Adelphi University.

It was evident from my survey that many faculty and some students felt the situation at their own schools was rapidly approaching such a point. A large proportion of the replies reflected a distinct uneasiness with the increasing role of athletics in prep school life. It is an issue about which no one active in teaching at these institutions can be unaware.

For those readers unfamiliar with prep school ways, it must again be noted that, in most cases, faculty members also are expected to coach a team sport. This may involve all three seasons: fall, winter, and spring. There also are personnel hired primarily or entirely as coaches and who are affiliated with their schools' athletic departments; such persons usually have majored in physical education and are well-qualified to coach. While every effort is made to match the individual with a sport with which he or she may have at least some familiarity, this is often not possible. My husband recalls being tossed into the lion's den of sophomore soccer in the fall of his first year of prep school teaching at Mount Hermon. He had never seen a soccer game and so found himself running up and down the field with a whistle in his mouth without the least idea of when to blow it or why. Fortunately, he was paired with an extremely patient teacher-coach who knew the game. In the spring he found himself coaching baseball, a sport that he loathed. Only during the winter season, when he coached basketball, was he able to regain at least some respect from the students concerning his coaching and athletic ability.

As for myself, I vividly remember being interviewed and hired for a teaching position by Cushing Academy's headmaster, the late Clarence P. Quimby, in my laboratory at the Woods Hole Oceanographic Institute in Massachusetts. After my academic responsibilities had been clarified, he announced, almost as an afterthought, that I would be the varsity girls swimming coach, "since you have been in Woods Hole, are a marine biologist, and can swim" — a *non sequitur* that still gives me pause. Fortunately, I had an excellent swimmer on the team who also happened to be the athletic director's daughter, and she was very helpful in teaching me how to coach. I could never have survived without her. It turned out to be a wonderful learning experience and one that provided an excellent way to get to know students outside the classroom. Furthermore, embodied in the art of good coaching are the skills of good teaching, the ability to take students from where they are and move them to a level of proficiency consonant with the fullest expression of their abilities.

The heavy involvement of prep school academic faculty in coaching intensifies student-faculty interaction and goes a long way toward establishing a feeling of community. It is absolutely astounding how many prep school alumni remain interested in who won such big rivalry football games as Andover-Exeter, Deerfield-Northfield Mount Hermon,* or Kent-Loomis Chaffee, especially when one considers that virtually all went on to college and thus might have been expected to transfer their loyalties to their respective alma maters. The psychological reasons for this are undoubtedly complex, but they cannot be unrelated to one factor that is undoubtedly one of athletics' most valuable contribution to prep school life — its attention to each student.

Far more than is possible at a public school, many, if not most, prep school students have the opportunity to be on a team that competes with teams of equal strength from other schools. In addition to the usual varsity and junior varsity teams in the various sports, a

---

*A member of the administration at Deerfield Academy informed me in no uncertain terms that, for Deerfield, this was definitely not "the big game," but rather one with a school higher on the elitist scale. The reasons for this are almost certainly those discussed in Chapter 4, because the close proximity of the Deerfield and Northfield Mount Hermon campuses in northwestern Massachusetts would otherwise make them logical "big game" rivals.

prep school also might build such competitive teams as "C squad" (juniors and seniors not good enough for the varsity), "junior league" (mostly sophomores), and "midget" (mostly first-year students). Most of the students involved will go on to colleges and universities where their athletic ability is not at a level required for intercollegiate sports. It is therefore not surprising that they look back with affection — and often give financial support — to the one education institution that provided them that opportunity.

To understand the genuine dilemma that athletics presents at the prep school, the fact that virtually all faculty are expected to coach must be paired with the fact that success in competitive athletics is a large drawing card for alumni financial support and also represents a big factor in bringing the schools to the attention of prospective students and their parents.

Unfortunately, this pairing of academic faculty coaching with the pressure for successful (that is, winning) athletic programs often directly affects the hiring of academic faculty. Understandably, athletic departments find it in their best interest to communicate to the administration the sports for which they need coaches. Because the financial welfare of the school is one of their major responsibilities, headmasters, in turn, may be inclined to choose persons who fill their schools' coaching needs over those who may be better qualified to deal with the academic subject they are being hired to teach. Whether this practice is widespread or occurs in only a few isolated cases is less important than the perception. A large percentage of the faculty sample viewed this practice as standard procedure. Many respondents voiced strong feelings that its effect was to cheapen the value of the academic mission for which the schools were originally established.

I can understand this feeling. At one school where I taught, I attended a reception to open the school academic year. I was introduced to a new faculty member hired to teach English. As the man could not speak English without numerous grammatical errors, goodness knows how he could have taught students to write properly. The headmaster's general introduction of new faculty later solved the mystery: The new English teacher also would coach a major varsity sport. I have sent quizzes to be photocopied on the science department machine only to be told that it was in use copying lacrosse play diagrams. I recall one year in which two faculty members did not attend the first science department meeting of the academic year because they were out on the athletic fields. The excuse provided later was that the person responsible for scheduling had caused the conflict, and doubtless this explanation was correct. However, the important issue is the choice made by the two teachers as to which was the more important — in one case, the athletic involvement was not even a regularly scheduled team function. Such value choices on the part of faculty are not lost on either their colleagues or their students and, accurately or not, reflect badly on the priorities of the school. Worse, the absences were accepted without question by the department chairperson. From my survey of the faculties of other schools, it seems that such attitudes are widespread throughout the prep school world.

One way the influence of athletics on the prep school curriculum might be diminished would be to place more power in the hands of the various academic departments, especially when it comes to selecting candidates. At many schools, a prospective teacher of an academic subject may be interviewed by the chair of the athletics department. Under such a system, neither I nor my husband, who was recognized for teaching excellence both at Mount Hermon and Wesleyan University, would have been hired. If the selection process went through the academic department only and it is made clear by the administration which priority come first, it might help ensure that the candidates' qualifications for teaching a subject are placed ahead of the sports they can coach. But such a plan would work only if the chairpersons of the academic departments were fully supported by the administration.

Probably the sharpest and most direct conflicts between the academic and athletic spheres of prep school life occur in the classroom. Because prep school interscholastic competition often involves lengthy intrastate or even interstate travel, team members must be excused from classes. Thus teachers find their demanding academic schedule further burdened with make-up work, especially if a test is missed and a new one has to be composed for only one or two absent students. I have known of students released from classes to attend a three-day "hockey conference" in Chicago and final exams rescheduled so as not to conflict with meets. Such incidents are common and often unavoidable. Many faculty simply do not bother to reschedule tests or laboratories for the missing students. But by so doing, they show students, athletes and nonathletes alike, the emptiness of their school's claim to put academics first. Such practices also help to increase hostility toward athletics on the part of academic faculty less enamored with the glory of sports.

Still another area of annoyance expressed by the prep school faculty members in my survey was that they must often cover the classes of faculty coaches so that those faculty members can accompany their teams on road trips. Considering the heavy teaching load of prep school teachers, this is no small burden. Even more galling, noncoaching faculty members may be asked to cover the classes of other faculty members so that those teachers can attend coaching "clinics." As one faculty member put it:

> It would be one thing if I had to cover my colleagues' classes so they could attend a meeting related to the professional interests for which they were *presumably* hired. But *damn* it pisses me off that I must do so just so they can go off and play coach!

This last comment pinpoints a growing problem: the placing of faculty coaching skill development ahead of academic responsibilities. I have arranged for scientists to talk to members of our department only to have some skip the lecture to attend aerobics classes or "coaching exams." Especially in such fields as science, where the material is changing constantly, this shift in priorities results almost inevitably in subject-matter obsolescence. The reputation of an entire department may suffer as a result. More than a few faculty members, hired initially as academics, have found the personal rewards of coaching far greater than those provided by the heavy demands of classroom teaching. Increasing attention then gets paid to "coaching strategies" and the reading of coaching journals. Often this enthusiasm for coaching even extends to the teacher's wardrobe. While most faculty coaches are content to wear sweat pants or shorts, those enamored of the job may wear outfits that outdo professionals in their sophistication. Far from decrying this trend, some schools take pride in it. In the Phillips Andover Academy 1987 annual report, the school's athletics director wrote:

> More and more . . . the love of their sports has taken our coaches to expertise. Membership in coaching associations and clinic attendance has helped a great deal.

For faculty much of this may merely reflect a desire for emulating athletic prowess never actually achieved in real life. It also further provides a psychological feeling of being "one of the boys," or girls. Such behavior tends to be characteristic of younger faculty who, after all, may often be as little as five or six years older than some of their charges. In one incident related to me, a female coach who had for years courted first-name-basis chumminess with students, on getting married suddenly decided that she was an adult. A hapless student who failed to notice the metamorphosis found himself doing push-ups for calling her by her first name.

In the context of the strong emphasis on winning, another incident is pertinent and revealing. A student was told by her parents that they did not want her to participate in a varsity interscholastic contest because she had a high fever. In a decision they later came to regret, they allowed her to attend the event as a spectator but gave her explicit instructions to inform the coach of her illness and their decision that she could not compete. The parents were shocked when they learned later that their daughter *had* competed. When questioned, she said that she had told the coach of her illness and her parents wishes but was informed that she had to participate anyway.

The parents were furious. Notes to the coach demanding an explanation went unanswered. Finally, confronted directly by the mother, the coach denied having seen the student before the event or having talked with her to learn that she was sick. The parents confronted their daughter with this statement, and the daughter stuck by her story, backed up by another student. Clearly, one of the two was lying. A long time would pass before the issue was resolved. The following season the daughter broke a bone at an unsupervised practice (for obvious safety reasons, strictly against the school rules). In the ensuing investigation, in dealing with a reference made by the girl's father to the earlier incident, the coach made a slip that made it clear who had lied and, when pressed, so admitted in a handwritten letter of apology to the parents.

This incident might have been dangerous or even fatal for the student involved. To be generous one could attribute it to the young coach's immaturity. However, the coach may well have been the victim of a win-at-any-cost school atmosphere. Success in the sport involved had brought much favorable publicity to both coach and school, a factor that any dismissal would obviously endanger. Unfavorable publicity is an absolute anathema to all prep schools. As far as the parents heard, the coach got not even a reprimand, despite the fact that a student caught lying in such a serious matter would certainly have been suspended and quite possibly expelled. This double standard was not lost on those students aware of the case. The entire matter suggests symptoms of a disproportionate importance given to successful athletics by the school involved.*

Another incident also is symbolically important. At one school where I taught, two varsity coaches lied to their team about the actual score in a meet, thereby leading its members to feel as if they needed to expend only a bit more energy to win. As it turned

---

*Some years later I learned that the school head was privy to personal information concerning the young coach that influenced the decision-making process, and the head very much regretted the way the matter was handled in terms of leaving the parents in the dark. Unfortunately, for the students involved, including several besides the victim who also knew the truth, the message conveyed was one of institutional hypocrisy. A reviewer of my manuscript (also a former school head) pointed out that the law often protects teachers from being dismissed for lying, a protection less available to students.

out, though considerably further behind than they had been told, they won. Not only was the lie left unchallenged, it was proclaimed with pride in the school's alumni magazine when the tale was told in a student essay. The essay had been written as an English assignment for a teacher-coach who, missing the incongruity, submitted it to the alumni magazine.

To put this story into proper context, I must again note that prep schools portray themselves as institutions involved in "inculcating values." At the same time the article appeared, the headmaster had just stated publicly that "deliberate dishonesty would not be tolerated" at the school. If a school head states that deliberate dishonesty will not be tolerated and his school then proudly publicizes a victory gained by it, the message to students is clear: deliberate dishonesty is not to be tolerated — unless you are a winning coach.

One can, of course, argue that, because the motivations in this case were benevolent ones, the lies were harmless. But were they? During the same academic year a student who had lied to protect a close friend from being expelled on suspicion of drug use was himself expelled. He defended his actions on precisely the same grounds. Across the board, it was the number-one perception among both the faculty and students in my sample that, in athletics and elsewhere, such practices of proclaiming one thing but doing another were standard operating procedures at their schools. Concerning what is *said* by the schools about athletics versus academics and what is actually the case, it is often the students, rather than the faculty, who perceive a double standard. The 19 April 1986 Loomis Chaffee student newspaper noted that a weekend schedule of two varsity team sports made it impossible for team members to study for exams. What was one head coach's "compromise solution"? Schedule no exams at these times.

Both students and faculty in my sample also noted a double standard in the widespread use of postgraduate "ringers" to beef up the varsity sports programs. Graduates of public high schools and often on full scholarships, these postgraduates, or PGs, often are subjected to snobbish, behind-the-back comments from both students and faculty about their level of intelligence as compared with those who went through the normal admission procedures. While this perception is unjust and in most cases incorrect, there is little doubt that, were it not for their athletic ability, such post-graduates would not have been admitted and they, their peers, and the faculty know it. An article in a 1986 issue of the *Log,* the Loomis Chaffee student newspaper, titled "A Tribute to the PGs," specifically lists only the athletic contributions of each student (all males). The article concludes by saying that "the entire school is grateful to them for keeping up the winning tradition at Loomis Chaffee." As appalling as the article was in terms of how these young men were perceived, one must admire its candor concerning just why they were there. Few other schools would be this honest. Of course, the author, it must be remembered, was a student; and students generally share no illusions on this matter. Nor do the students fail to spot the faculty and administration's value systems on these and related issues.

As the first of these student articles noted, seniors deemed worthy by the faculty of being in charge of the students on their dormitory floors are almost inevitably athletes. A student respondent to my survey noted:

> By appointing prefects for athletic reasons, and sacrificing academics and other extracurriculars, the system over-emphasizes athletics and underemphasizes academics, the primary reason for coming to an institution like [this school].

My faculty survey did not include school heads, so it is only fair to insert a comment by one former headmaster who reviewed my manuscript. He noted:

> There is much about athletics in boarding schools at least that bothers me. Although, when I think about it, I have the same opinion about athletics across the secondary school spectrum. I believe we spend too much time in practices and uninterrupted seasons. Interestingly enough, though, all efforts I made to get the school to limit athletic practices to, say, an hour and a quarter or an hour and a half at most were

defeated by the faculty. I even got support from the trustees (mostly alumni) but it was the faculty that was unshakable. This is not unrelated to the story you tell of the faculty complaining about athletics but then proceeding to pick prefects who were all athletes.

At this point, should any school abandon the policy of bringing in PGs to beef up athletic teams, its widespread use by rival schools would almost inevitably mean a disastrous season. Thus a practice that ideally provides an excellent educational opportunity for the postgraduate is tainted by its widespread perception of being a hypocritical, win-at-any-cost endeavor. One school, which used ringers quite liberally, became known for many years for its headmaster's Sunday morning review of the school's athletic teams' successes of the preceding week. Athletes were shifted from team to team to ensure that, if any team lost, it would not do so again when it met the same rival later in the season. Such practices lend further fuel to the flames of suspicion concerning an overemphasis on winning.*

It is difficult to know where the blame lies for this heavy stress on athletics. To be fair, the prep school is doing nothing more than reflecting the current national craze concerning sports. Furthermore, with some notable exceptions, prep schools often excel in helping students place sports defeats in their proper perspective. Yet there are disturbing signs for the future. In the past even overly enthusiastic pep rally banners deemed possibly offensive to an opponent were censored by the prep school administrations. During the 1950s at Mount Hermon School the slogan, "Cream the Green" (referring to the colors of arch-rival Deerfield Academy), was ruled too offensive. Now the lid is off: "Kill Kent" banners swing uncensored. A 21 February 1987 front-page article in the student newspaper of Kent School publicized an

---

*Sometimes, the practice gets out of hand. At one prep school several postgraduates accustomed to the personal freedom of public school and chafing under prep school rules managed to terrorize their young coach and to extort additional special privileges from him. Attempts to correct the situation led to further intimidation and violence.

upcoming hockey meet with a nonleague rival by quoting a team member's description of the game as "always very emotional, because we have had many conflicts in the past. We don't like them and they don't like us." In another article concerning an athletic event between two prep schools, parents were described as verbally abusing officials and cheering the outbreak of fighting. It is not surprising that their offspring refused to shake the hands of members of the winning team, for years a mark of "good sportsmanship."

It would be unjust to imply that all, or even most, prep school athletic departments condone such behavior. Yet they and their school administrations often create a climate that makes poor sportsmanship almost inevitable. As the schools constantly point out, it is the faculty coaches who are the role models for proper behavior. The chair of one school's athletic department wrote a memo to the faculty to explain why class absences for athletics occur. He stressed the *need* for such competitiveness:

> The athletic facilities and inter-scholastic programs at schools like: Hotchkiss, Choate, Andover, Exeter, Lawrenceville, Hill, Taft, and NMH [Northfield Mount Hermon] clearly demonstrates [sic] that quality schools place a high priority on excellence in athletics. Since we are trying to attract the same student and our athletic facilities cannot compare with these schools, it is essential that we offer a competitive athletic program.

According to the "academics first" value claimed by all of these schools, one should argue precisely the opposite. Any student or parent who looks at a college preparatory school's athletic facilities and schedule as a criterion for selecting it is probably one that most of the academic faculty would prefer went elsewhere. It is doubtful that many parents select an Andover or Exeter for their athletic schedules or facilities, grand as they may be. In responding to the memo, I wrote:

> If it is true that "our athletic facilities cannot compare to these schools," as I see it there are two alternatives. One is

to divert funds into an insane spending spiral so as to outdo these "BEST SCHOOLS" in athletic grandeur. So doing would certainly put us in step with the national sports mania. But rather than following, why not try *leading*? I am betting that if, with an appropriate amount of publicity, [we] announced that [we were] dropping out of the prep school athletics arms race your memo suggests exists and, since it now possesses more-than-adequate though not pretentious athletic facilities, that it would henceforth direct all of its development funds toward the improvement of its academic program and facilities, we would be advertising a feature of great attractiveness to parents of just the sort of student that we *and* the "BEST SCHOOLS" would want. Indeed, as we move more and more into the boarding school realm [author's note: the school then had large numbers of day students and was in the process of increasing its proportion of boarders], now might be absolutely the best time to so state, and thus, for the right reasons, *we* might become THE "BEST SCHOOL."

Despite my call for open discussion on this issue, my memo (sent, as was the athletic department chairperson's memo, to all members of the administration and faculty) received no reply. Nor did it receive any recognition from the administration. Although several faculty members, either by direct comments or personal notes, expressed strong support for my position, only one did so publicly. Another was going to send (anonymously) copies of my memo to all of the school's trustees. Whether he actually did so, I do not know. As I noted previously, it is not at all unusual at college preparatory schools for faculty to be afraid to speak out openly.

What has happened here? To those readers whose image of New England college preparatory schools is one of high school Harvards, it must be a shock to learn of them behaving more like the stereotypical universities whose football players can do anything with a football except autograph it. How could it happen that jackets were purchased for members of a college preparatory school's swim team when they won the New Englands yet its equally successful mathematics team was denied even T-shirts? It would appear that, not only have prep schools failed to lead in the search for a cure for our nation's current sports insanity, they have instead fallen victim to it.

Why? One answer is suggested by author James McLachlan in his book, *American Boarding Schools: A Historical Study*. McLachlan quotes an early 20th century headmaster:

> Athletics are of the utmost importance in establishing righteousness in the school . . . for controlling moral evil you have got to consider the care of the body and the best thing for a boy to do is to work hard and then after a short interval to play hard and then to work hard again and then to play hard again and then, when the end of the day has come, to be so tired that he wants to go to bed and sleep. That is the healthy and good way for a boy to live. (1970, p. 285)

McLachlan expresses his opinion that "The logic of the passage seems to be that athletics were a substitute for sex, the playing field a surrogate for the bed." It was astounding to me to find that, among the prep school faculty respondents to my random survey (which asked for *their* interpretations of the same passage), more than half of the respondents found themselves in essential agreement with McLachlan, whose opinions I also sent along to them. The only real disagreement came from a person who labeled the statement "Bullshit!" (This same person also confessed, however, to being his school's athletic director.)

Most prep schools have progressed beyond the naive and rather puritanical view of students exemplified by the headmaster's comment cited by McLachlan. Yet, independent of the obvious health benefits of exercise to developing bodies, the absence of an extensive athletic program in boarding prep schools would be considered disastrous. As one respondent of 20 years' teaching experience put it:

> A lovely quote. I believe he was at Andover [author's note: This is incorrect. The statement was made by the Reverend Endicott Peabody, Groton's most revered headmaster.]

> There is little doubt that [prep school] athletic programs are designed to keep the kids busy — otherwise they would be in the dorms doing you-know-what! Whether it is as obvious anti-sex as it was in the 19th century is another question, but there is still a lot of "health body-healthy mind" sort of thinking around.

As this comment and my sample suggests, many prep school faculty view athletics as a valuable time-filler to keep the students out of mischief, sexual or otherwise. In expressing his strong agreement with McLachlan's statement in describing the unstated views of his school, another person wrote:

> The ideal athlete (and a very high percent of students) is involved in interscholastic sports [and] seems to be a sexless sort of creature. . . . The more vocal the coach about the value of athletics (muscular Christianity updated), the more his or her athletes approach the androgynous ideal.

Another individual, reflecting a theme expressed by many respondents, admitted that:

> The school schedules time very tightly so that there is very little free time. The faculty seems to be afraid of what the students would do if allowed any freedom.

Still another went right to the heart of the matter by writing:

> Parents send their children to boarding schools to become disciplined, achievement-oriented, competitive and industrious. Traditionally, they view sex as a recreational activity, not a productive one. Yes, I believe most prep schools foster McLachlan's comments.

Yet another, in response to being asked if he agreed with McLachlan, wrote: "Most definitely. As a product of an all-boys' school and a teacher at two coed schools, I would say this still rings true."

It should be reemphasized that these responses represent the feelings of a statistically significant majority of the respondents.

That more than half of my prep school faculty colleagues viewed their school's athletic program as "keep-'em-busy" babysitting is a result that I found staggering. Even 5% would have surprised me. Yet it is quite likely correct that, were it not for athletics, dormitory life for faculty residents would be intolerable. Nor, in truth, is the ethic of constant "busy-ness" limited to using the athletic program for this purpose. Other activities also seem to be scheduled with the view that student leisure time would be a potential threat to school tranquillity. Undoubtedly the Protestant work ethic is reflected here. As one respondent put it:

> Our students' time is overscheduled but not necessarily because we (consciously) subscribe to the code of that nine-teenth century headmaster [The statement was made in the early 20th century]. A majority of students here play inter-scholastic sports; a majority is involved in some extracurric-ular activity; all students participate in the work program, performing assigned and scheduled jobs for 4-5 hours a week. When you add classes, study halls, meetings, dorm closing, etc., of course the students and faculty members will feel overscheduled. But this situation has resulted from the school's missionary tradition, its size, its desire to be flexible (ironic, huh?) and open to students' needs and wishes, and its unwritten credo that there is something wrong with you if you are not overworked and tired.

This last comment suggests that athletics are viewed as merely another aspect of the work ethic. Another respondent made this view still more explicit. In support of the minority disagreeing with McLachlan, he wrote: "Athletics isn't play . . . it's part of the work due to the obligatory nature of athletics. 'Play' is after work."

Because only those students in the sample who volunteered to be interviewed (in person or by mail) were given an opportunity to comment on the headmaster's statement and McLachlan's reaction to it, those results were less definitive. It was clear, how-ever, that there was some support for the faculty majority view:

> I feel they did keep us busy in order to keep us under con-trol. If you are tired you are not going to get into trouble.
> This [idea] most definitely did prevail at [name of school]. Actually, it was a big faculty debate at [name of

school] before the merger [to become coed] . . . how to tire
them out so they would not fool around. In the end, the more
rigorous athletic schedule at the boy's school was kept so
they would wear out the guys.

Two other students commented that, if athletics *were* considered as a means of controlling student sexual activity, they were
certainly a massive failure at it.

In all fairness to athletics, they are not the only activity that
may play the role of the tail wagging the dog. While I was teaching at Northfield Mount Hermon, the choir, led by an incredibly
popular and talented director, was the big publicity-getter. The
idea of a member of the elite *a cappella* choir missing a trip to
sing for an alumni group for a mere class was unthinkable. One
learned to accept choir rehearsal absences from academic appointments. The problem became particularly acute during preparations for the annual Spring Sacred Concert. At these times the
entire student body of both campuses joined together for a massive hymn sing. Held in a huge auditorium built originally for
school founder Dwight L. Moody's revival meetings, the concert
was as beautiful as its rehearsal schedule was disruptive to normal school life during the preceding weeks. To complain about
football interrupting academics was one thing; to do so about
Sacred Concert was to risk a reputation like that of Ebenezer
Scrooge. Just as the athletic department might tell the school
admissions department of their needs for next year ("linemen,
please; we're okay in the backfield") so, too, might the choir
director point out a lack of basses or sopranos, or the orchestra
leader complain about a surplus of brasses and a deficiency of
woodwinds.

Athletics also came in for some hard knocks from survey
respondents concerning sexism. Two questions raised this issue.
One asked, "If your school is coed, do you feel the programs (i.e.,
academic, athletic, social, etc.) are equal for both males and
females?" The other asked, "Are there instances of sexism on the
part of faculty members or students?" Many responses identified
the athletic programs as the major reservoir of the sex discrimi-

nation still existing on campus. Even those who felt things were basically equal found fault here. One female faculty member of 12 years' experience wrote:

> Equal . . . although it's only in the last two years that a female trainer has been hired and that girls have been allowed in the training room. In terms of attitude, the school (including the students) tends to place more importance on boys' athletics, despite the fact that, year after year, the girls' teams are more successful.

Another faculty member of 25 years commented: "I feel there is goodwill, but unconscious sexism remains. An example is the stress on women performing in athletics as proof of equality."

Not surprisingly, far more females than males detected sexism in school practices. But one male faculty member of 20 years, after denying sexism existed, commented that there was "some reverse sexism by women."

Again, to be fair, the move to coeducation generally meant that the females moved onto formerly all-male campuses. As a result, athletic departments found themselves having to adapt facilities designed for males to serve the needs of both sexes, at times a nearly impossible task. Furthermore, the departments often were staffed with personnel who had spent the major portion of their professional lives as trainers dealing with only males. When one considers the relative speed with which coeducation took place, it is perhaps a wonder that they have done as well as they have.

One woman faculty member of 11 years, after pointing out that things were "definitely not [equal] in athletics; those [female] sports are tolerated because if not the girls would be elsewhere causing trouble," then went on to include her entire school faculty, including the females, as part and parcel of the sexism problem. This indictment of female faculty in knowingly or unknowingly acquiescing to male chauvinism was repeated by several faculty respondents. In a long and very thoughtful letter, one female faculty member joined several others in including many of their female students in this group as well.

The importance of this last perception simply cannot be over-emphasized. It is an issue to which I will direct considerable attention in a later chapter. In the present context, however, one occurrence is worth noting. My own request for on-campus housing so that I could devote more time to work with some interested women faculty members in developing a program to deal directly with the school's admitted sexuality- and gender-related problems among both students and faculty was refused. The reason? I could no longer coach a sport.

CHAPTER 6

Sex, Values, and the Prep School Faculty

"The school rule book states that the student should be mature enough to refrain from sexual contact! The policy was that [if caught] you should go for counseling. . . . They shouldn't treat sex as if it were dirty or wrong!"

— Student respondent

My questionnaire left space for the student respondents to comment on anything they wished about the sexual attitudes, behavior, and values they perceived as being conveyed by their schools. Most took advantage of this opportunity to vent often bitter feelings against the faculty and their school administrations.

As a former prep school faculty member, this was especially discouraging for me to read. I felt that the students were presenting an unfair caricature of my views and those of most of my colleagues. I wanted to discount what I was reading and dismiss it as mere adolescent sour grapes. But I could not. For one, the opinions were widely shared. For another, almost all were presented with a maturity and sensitivity that was most impressive. In no case was a sense of dislike for their schools conveyed. Instead, the students gave the impression of feeling let down by them. This impression was reinforced by those I interviewed in person. All were perceptive, interesting, and interested. I might feel, as I did at times, that their perceptions were wrong. But right or wrong, these *were* their perceptions; and I felt strongly that they deserved full attention.

It was the result of reading these discouraging student comments that led me to contact my prep school faculty colleagues at the schools involved in my research. *Were* our policies hypocritical, more interested in school image than reality? I needed to know. The faculty replies provided no comfort. To a surprisingly large degree (and, in most cases, a statistically significant one) the negative perceptions of the students concerning the way their schools viewed sexuality were shared by those who taught in them.

One question asked if the respondent knew of cases of sexual activity between students and faculty members. Both faculty and students agreed that it was uncommon but did happen. One female student wrote:

> I had a relationship with a married male teacher and then broke up with him. A year after this relationship, I won an award at the end of my senior year but the female director of the school found out about this relationship with the male teacher, fired him and asked me to give back the award! I was called into her office and asked personal questions and was dealt with in an immature way. I didn't know how to deal with it, and spent time after the affair in therapy. The director then said I could keep the award — to date I have not yet seen it.

Overlooking the insensitive manner in which this matter appears to have been handled, I know of no school with any written policy on student-faculty relationships, possibly because it lies beyond their comprehension that such a thing could happen. Yet such relationships have occurred at all of the schools at which I taught, as they have at most (and perhaps all) of the 16 schools included in my sample. Three incidents related to me by survey respondents should suffice to illustrate this point:

> One young female faculty member is known among the students to have had an ongoing affair with a senior male student. He was seen frequently coming out of her apartment in the early morning. Whether all campus faculty knew about this or not I do not know. He is now in college and she attends his athletic events. So it is not always the male fac-

ulty member with the female student as one assumes. This of course does exist.

***

A young male faculty member at our school was carrying on with a senior student. Everyone on campus knew this, except the headmaster . . . or at least he claimed to some after the event that he did not. This faculty member moved out of the dormitory into another faculty member's home. The faculty member and student would go away weekends. His wife would sign out the senior student. This was allowed and hushed up. The student graduated. At the end of the year, the faculty member left for graduate school. His wife and child left for another private school. They eventually divorced. His wife has now left teaching.

***

I remember an older faculty member at our school who became very fond of a senior. He had her in class. This faculty member and student were seen together frequently on campus. It was learned afterwards that she would leave the dormitory after lights out and meet him. After she graduated, they married. Her family was most unhappy about the relationship and with the school for allowing it to occur.

Certainly, this is an area in which schools *should* have a policy. They should do so not because of the age difference (our society is "age-ist" enough as it is) and not because sex is wrong, but because the power versus no-power status separating faculty and students means that such relationships cannot be equal ones and thus are bound to be exploitative. Exploitation is factor on which schools must focus in regulating personal interactions of any sort. Unfortunately, it is a term I have yet to read in any prep school rule book in the context of sexual behavior or, for that matter, in any other context. An "any other" case in point was a 1980s Choate-Rosemary Hall and Emma Willard School drug bust that came to light with the arrest in New York's John F. Kennedy Airport of a Choate-Rosemary Hall day student who had attempted to smuggle in some $300,000 worth of cocaine. Subsequent investigation uncovered extensive student involvement, and eventually more than 40 students from both schools were expelled. Much to the schools' chagrin, the incident sparked sufficient interest to rate a segment on the CBS news documentary, *60 Minutes*. Even allowing for the videotape editing necessary for such television programs, the Choate-Rosemary Hall headmaster's words to the assembled students shown on the *60 Minutes* program seemed concerned mostly with how the school would be perceived by the outside world. However, it should not have been the damage to schools' image or the drugs that were the central issue. Rather, the issue was that wealthy students who could afford to buy the drugs saw nothing wrong in allowing a scholarship day student, eager for their acceptance, to travel to South America to do their dangerous dirty work for them. This was exploitation, pure and simple. That so few school personnel seemed to have grasped this fact marks much of the real tragedy of the Choate-Rosemary Hall/Emma Willard drug-bust incident.

In response to the question, "What is your perception of the amount of sexual activity between single faculty members?" the faculty responses varied from "very little" to "a lot." One replied, "a very healthy quota!" while another quipped, "not enough!" Most felt that the heavy faculty workload acted to keep such activity at a low level. Single faculty members often had relationships with persons outside their schools.

More interesting were answers given to the question, "What would be the reaction of your school if a male and female faculty member decided they wanted to live together without getting married?" Here, once again, the sexist double standard reared its ugly head:

> Young male "bachelor" teachers get a more tolerant view than do their female counterparts. Both fellow faculty and students judge female behavior more harshly than they do male activity.

By far the most common responses were "no way," "would not condone it," "not allowed," "termination if not tenured; if tenured, God knows," and so on. In the only three non-negative responses, two used the term "tolerant," the third, "accepting." Those reporting negative responses on the part of their schools made it plain that the schools would become involved in their faculty couples' personal lives to resolve the "problem":

> The couple is strongly encouraged to get married . . . no couple has ever lived together for more than six months without succumbing to this pressure.
>
> ***
>
> Unmarried faculty could live together for one or two years, then they had to make a decision as to whether they were going to get married or leave the school.
>
> ***
>
> This could only happen here after their engagement were [sic] announced.
>
> ***
>
> No way. It is not allowed and it is all made quite clear. Marry first — then live together.
>
> ***
>
> One male faculty member whose "mate" was not part of the school community was told that she had to get her own apartment off campus or he would be fired.

This last comment suggests what a vast majority of the respondents admitted: It made a difference where the couple resided.

> It is not possible if the faculty members are living in a dormitory. A lover is allowed to "visit" — not clear how long the visit can be.
>
> ***
>
> It is NOT allowed in the dormitories. Outside dormitories, I'm not sure. Discretion is highly recommended.
>
> ***
>
> I think the reaction would be that this would be fine as long as certain appearances were maintained — separate addresses, for example. I think it's been done, but unofficially.
>
> ***
>
> We've switched around on this: said "no," then said (to two Ph.D.s), well, okay, since you're not in a dorm.

This is just a sample of such responses. The suggested sanctioning of hypocrisy as school policy is not lost on the students. They are perfectly aware of what is going on. In response to the same question, one student wrote:

> It wouldn't be allowed. One teacher had been living with her boyfriend in college — when they joined the faculty they had to live in separate dorms. However, *off campus* two teachers had been living together for about eight years before marrying. The school didn't appear to mind that . . . out of sight, out of mind.

It is not only the students who were aware of this hypocrisy. Some faculty hinted at it. For example:

> I knew of one couple that got away with it (living together without being married) by swapping visits back and forth. He would come to live with her and then she would come to live with him. . . .

Another was more explicit on this point:

> School would not condone two people living together who were not married. However, exceptions were made if a faculty member was not living on campus. One woman made it clear that she was not going to allow the school to dictate her choices, and also made it clear that the relationship was more important to her than the job. She "won," but felt it was only because her lover was a graduate of the school and had been a "BWoC" [author's note: "big wheel on campus"] athlete. She felt that such a hypocritical attitude was a loss to the student body.

So it was. What are they learning instead? The reply of one faculty member to the question suggests an answer: "It is not allowed. If they are dorm people they are chastised. If they live out of the dorm, people pretend they don't know. Some lie about being married."

In reading this, I was reminded of one of my student respondents who wrote, very simply but powerfully: "[Name of school] taught me how to lie." With that comment in mind it struck me as ironic to read the comment of the faculty member who wrote: "[The school] would not allow it, since it does not set an acceptable standard for our youth."

From my many years in prep school teaching, I am familiar with opinions such as those expressed in the last comment and, at one time, probably held them myself. Now I wonder. What "acceptable standard" were we really conveying? On this unmarried-faculty-living-together issue, I now find myself in complete agreement with the teacher with 15 years of boarding school life behind her who wrote:

> Strong disapproval [of unmarried living together]. The school imagines itself to be a role model of ideal behavior. It often is but not in the ways it thinks and the ways it is are often far from ideal.

Far from ideal, indeed. There is a genuine intellectual dishonesty in forcing people to live two lives — their normal relationship life off campus and another, "pretend" one on campus. By so doing, the schools *are* providing a role model. But it is hardly an admirable one. The students spot such duplicity instantly.

I suppose I always sensed this. It was not until I did the survey, however, that I discovered how perceptive students really are. The effect on faculty forced to live this deceit is almost certainly equally negative. One especially moving comment perhaps says it all:

> As a single faculty member involved in a long term [four years] relationship with another [name of school] teacher I was shocked and angered that the school considered that it had the right to dictate to me who I could or couldn't have as visitors in my own apartment. [About living together] I wouldn't have wanted to, but I didn't think they should be disapproving if I chose to spend time in his apartment or he in mine. We were a serious, committed couple who could have provided yet another positive role model to their students had we been allowed to act normally, instead of feeling that we, just like the students, had to "sneak around" in order to spend time together (our time was as tightly sched-

uled as the students'). It seemed unnatural and unrealistic
for the school to approve only of marriage as a role model
for these students, when for most of them that was a long
way off and in the meantime they had a lot to learn about
love, sex, the opposite sex, and relationships — certainly
ignoring the sexuality of the students doesn't make it go
away; hopefully, acknowledging it will help students to discover and accept their own ideals.

Sadly, in a personal note to me encouraging me in my work,
this respondent revealed that she had decided she could not lead
such a dishonest life and left the school. It is difficult not to see
this as a loss, both for her school and for the students with whom
she came in contact.

Another case was that of a female faculty member who lived
on campus for a time until she developed a relationship with a
male faculty member. She then moved off campus so they could
have privacy. The relationship blossomed and the couple married.
They were then "acceptable" and moved back on campus. Except
for the move to protect the school's image, the couple's relationship developed as will most of their students' future relationships.
Unfortunately, from the way this couple was described, I suspect
that they will project only the image the school wants. Thus the
dishonesty is compounded, first to their students and second to
themselves.

Several faculty members pointed out that their school policies
encourage behavior that flies in the face of the very values they
claim to be upholding. One person put it this way: "Oddly
enough, I think one–night stands would be more tolerated than
this situation" [living together unmarried].

Another faculty member of 16 years directed her comments
even more strongly to this point:

> Good for you. It is high time someone looked into this
> sadly neglected area of prep school life. The schools attempt
> to role-play a way of life that no longer exists (if, indeed, it
> ever did), and only the students, it seems to me, are bright
> enough to see through all this. Mind you, I love prep schools

— they have tremendous potential. Since becoming coed, they have moved a long way from the dark ages they once represented. . . . But in the area of sexuality, the faculty for the most part are at a loss to know what to do. Headmasters talk about the old-fashioned values, the students laugh, the faculty (some) do, too, behind their backs, but it makes the old alums and trustees who support the schools happy. Probably they believe it! It speaks well for your school that you have been encouraged rather than discouraged in this project. Probably your long experience is a factor; certainly any younger faculty members here would get into trouble unless their results were what the school wanted to hear, and perhaps an older one too. In my opinion, in their attempts to control (read, "eliminate") student sexual activity, the schools actually foster views of sex and sexuality that, even by their own standards, are highly undesirable.

The question, "What would be the reaction of your school toward a female faculty member who became pregnant and remained a single parent?" brought similar responses. A large majority were negative, ranging in intensity from "So long, sinner," "*very* uncomfortable," "contract would be terminated," to "nothing" or "supportive." Just as in the case of the singles cohabitation question, however, the issue of keeping it out of the public eye was seen as the most important factor in the formulation of their schools' responses to this situation:

> I am afraid it would be viewed as inappropriate for a faculty member of a school where teachers' private lives are a cornerstone of the school life. It would be considered controversial; bad for school image.

In dealing with this question and the responses to it, I recalled a comment one of my faculty respondents made to me in a different context: "The major issue is not [between the faculty] but rather breaks [between the] faculty versus administration." I confess I did not grasp the significance of this remark when I first read it. The pregnancy question seemed to bring its importance to light. In dealing with the amount of emotional support a single female faculty parent might expect to receive, one person wrote: "From the institution, none; continued support as a faculty member." I interpreted this to mean that the woman would receive greater tolerance and understanding from the faculty than the school administration. This interpretation was supported by the following comments:

> Yikes! I think the school would get a lot of pressure to fire her, but I would hope they would resist. Don't know.
>
> ***
>
> This would be hard to say. The faculty may be supportive personally, but the board and the headmaster probably would request resignation.
>
> ***
>
> Most of the faculty would be supportive of the colleague. The administration's reaction, once again, is tough to predict. I don't think it would approve, but I think the threat of faculty response would prevent the administration from disciplinary or condemnatory action.

The overall message may be an encouraging one. As insensitive and judgmental as most of the faculty perceived their schools' reactions would be, it seems that the faculty, left to its own devices, might be more compassionate. Furthermore, and *most* encouraging, the last response suggests that the faculty might even be willing to challenge the administration over such an issue. If this is correct, it suggests that more humane and honest school policies concerning a case such as this in particular, and sexuality in general, might well be framed if the faculty flexed its collective muscle. Of course, prep school faculty members range from liberal to conservative, and thus a unified front is unlikely. Furthermore, conservative faculty often have a selective advantage in receiving administrative appointments and, as a result, the conservatism may be self-perpetuating.

If these last few responses are any indication, there do appear to be cracks in the wall and at least some light shining through. Values *do* evolve, after all.

In the 19th and even early 20th century a child caught masturbating was sent for medical help. His or her hands might be tied or a painful device fitted to the genitals both as a punishment and to prevent further occurrences. Yet my question, "In general, what do you think a faculty member's response would be in discovering a student masturbating?" and then, "What would be your own response?" brought only one comment that indicated that any faculty members would feel, as did this person, that the act was "unconscionable" and that the student "lacked restraint." All other faculty respondents saw masturbation as being a perfectly natural behavior. Typical reactions were "tiptoe out," "embarrassment," "apologize for the intrusion," and so forth. With the single exception just noted, there were hardly even *traces* remaining of the earlier value system. One respondent even commented about her own personal growth:

> I think it [masturbation] a natural and healthy act, important for one's sexual development, but I'm sure I am in the minority on this. My childhood religion (I was a Catholic) taught that it was a sin, but I outgrew that silly thinking years ago.

Significantly, the stated feeling of this respondent that she was "in the minority on this" was shared by many. As I indicated previously, almost all of the faculty respondents viewed themselves as more tolerant and understanding than their colleagues. This suggests that if these issues were brought into the open, a healthier campus climate might well be the result. I should again stress that my sample did not include school heads or administrators, though the result might well have been the same.

The same "I'm more open-minded than they are" perception also was evident in responses to the questions, "What do you think a faculty member's response would be upon discovering two students engaged in heterosexual intercourse?" and "What would be your own response?" For example, many said that their colleagues would send the students to the dean for disciplinary action, whereas they would talk to the students about "responsible sexuality," for example, birth control. A few said they would feel embarrassed and that, as one put it, they had "violated privacy." Interestingly, the same out-of-sight, out-of-mind image consciousness again raised its head here; one faculty member admitted that he or she would ask the students to "save it for vacation, if you must indulge."

On the whole, however, most of the individual faculty members' responses were healthy ones, though the majority did indicate that they would send both students for counseling. Sending students off to counseling is a practice the schools might well wish to reevaluate. The students are certainly aware of it, and their reaction is precisely that of the student whose comments open this chapter. To them it means the faculty views adolescent sexual activity as symptomatic of mental illness. It may well be that the counseling is of the best sort, that is, nonjudgmental and concerned only about the relationship being nonexploitative and responsible. This is not the students' perception, however. It would probably be better if all faculty were given inservice training in dealing with such issues so they can handle the "counseling" themselves. So doing would spare the students having to endure the humiliation of having yet another party involved. One faculty respondent suggested just such an approach:

> Ask them to drop by [my] house one hour later. Talk to them about how uncomfortable it was to find them, etc. etc. Talk openly about how long they have known each other, what their plans for the future are, is the girl or the boy protected, etc. etc.

It is difficult to find fault with this approach. I suspect if it were school policy to encourage it, the student reactions described in the next chapter would never occur. By choosing to make sexual activity a matter for disciplinary action, the schools may be blocking communication in sexual matters between students and faculty. As one student pointed out, at his school the penalty was precisely the same as the one meted out for stealing. Students understandably hesitate to confide in someone with the power to ruin their school career. As one student put it:

> The person I talked to most about sex was [not a faculty member]. She did not think it bad that sex was on campus.

But communication with any faculty was blocked by the knowledge that they could bust you.

One faculty member who would not betray a student's trust and "bust" him or her was a person who obviously had considered thoughtfully the negative values she perceived her school was promoting about sexuality. In a letter enclosed along with her questionnaire, she wrote:

> Sexual intercourse was forbidden and there was a rule forbidding students from being in rooms in opposite-sex dormitories. Therefore, when students were caught in each other's rooms, that fact alone, and not what they were doing in the room, could be cause for dismissal. This rule bothered me because the school seemed to be afraid to come out and say what they really meant; they were afraid to confront the issue of sexuality itself. Although I don't know of any recent incidents in which students were "fired" (kicked out) on the sole basis of being in their girl/boyfriend's room, several students went before the discipline committee and were placed on probation; this was definitely considered a major offense. One of the best students in the school was forbidden from attending graduation or prize night (despite the fact that he was the recipient of several prizes) because his girlfriend had entered his room for twenty-five minutes. They had done nothing sexual and were completely honest about the situation when confronted by a dorm faculty member. They were very much in love, had been seeing each other for one and a half years and were seeking some privacy — obviously a mistake. . . . Adolescents need time alone with members of the opposite sex, whether they are only friends or whether they are lovers. It's unnatural to expect students to confine their relations to public places. It also means that one often comes across students in various stages of passionate encounters either on the school lawns in fall and spring or in darkened lounges in the classroom buildings in the winter. I found this rather embarrassing both for the students and for me, but somehow it was considered acceptable, while talking quietly with a member of the opposite

sex in one's own room was not. My first year at [name of school] the bookstore sold T-shirts which said on the front: "[name of school] is for lovers" and on the back "with no place to go." Very appropriate. Obviously this lack of privacy and the rules against visitors did not prevent students from finding places for sex. The school is surrounded by woods, and it was a well-known fact that in nice weather students would go "cruising" in the early morning hours. I know of more than one couple who managed to spend the night in each other's rooms on a fairly regular basis without getting caught. Ironically, one of the most popular spots on campus (at least in the winter) was the chapel. It was removed from the main corridors of the classroom building, it was dark, very few faculty members ever thought to look in, and, best of all, the high pew backs provided privacy to God knows how many couples.

To those outside the prep school world, much of this concern with sex undoubtedly seems silly or even bizarre. But prep schools, like public high schools, deal with students on their way to becoming men and women. I tend to believe that by constantly referring to their students as *girls* and *boys*, the schools forget that, if they have done their job well, they are producing young women and men. It is true that students enter the schools at ages when *girl* or *boy* are proper terms. But both students and faculty may be better served by using terms that look ahead and thus aid in developing a mature self-image.

College preparatory boarding schools consider themselves *in loco parentis* and, in a very real sense, they truly are. Nothing causes the cold sweat of administrative fear more than the mere *suggestion* of a parent's lawsuit for some perceived abrogation of these responsibilities on the part of the school. Beyond that, it is not only that most prep schools see themselves as being *in loco parentis,* but that *they decide what good parents should be.*

One student told me of an incident that illustrates this last point. Her parents, both college professors, had raised their children in a manner that provided them with a warm, supportive environment but one that also allowed them to make their own decisions as they matured. After two years of public school, their daughter was sent to a private prep school. She decided to go to Boston on one of the weekends she was allowed off campus and to stay with a male friend who was then in college. Her dorm counselor was shocked to learn of her overnight stay plans and insisted that she call her father. This in itself is not an unusual action and, in truth, a responsible one. More significant, however, was the counselor's response to the father's "Sure, why not?" Stunned, the counselor asked for his permission in writing. He thought it silly but complied. Later, when the student was going to spend the night with another friend, also male, the counselor again made her go through the same process. Finally the father, in exasperation, asked his daughter to list all the men with whom she might conceivably stay so he could sign a general release form. She did so and gave it to the counselor. As the student put it:

> The counselor was enraged. She implied that my father was irresponsible. In truth, he merely respected me and my judgment . . . the school did not. It was obvious sex was their big worry. Ironically, on my dorm floor, I was the only one to graduate still a virgin!

In his book, *The Elite Schools: A Profile of Prestigious Independent Schools*, L. Baird refers to this counselor's attitude and the attitude of her school as merely reflecting the puritanical background out of which the schools developed. Such schools, he writes, "seem to simultaneously exhibit a denial of sex and an obsession with sex." He points out that, historically, prep schools tried to segregate sexual activity out of existence by gender segregation. Now, with many of these same schools coeducational, they reveal their nervousness about sex, as Baird puts it, with "thickets of rules and restrictions" (1977, p. 28). Each school is in continual fear of legal liability for the welfare of its students, which leads to their stressing an often highly puritanical view of sex and sexuality. The inevitable result, as Baird notes, is that the role of faculty members in student value formation, school claims to the contrary, are rated very low by students. School historian James McLachlan writes:

> The major aim of the American boarding school has been to preserve the innocence of childhood into a pure and responsible maturity. At least since the 1820s, many rich Americans preferred to have sons educated in pastoral isolation, secure from the physical and moral corruption and temptations of an increasingly urbanized and industrialized society, in schools modeled on idealized "families" in which the child's "natural depravity" could be suppressed and his "naturally good" impulses carefully nurtured. (1970, pp. 13–14)

A chapter dealing with the rules that prep school faculties have devised to control their students' behavior could go on forever. I constantly run into people who attended prep schools who have choice vignettes to share that underline the points I have raised.

The ambiance today at the leading college preparatory schools is by no means as parochial in view as the preceding might imply. Like the society that surrounds them, prep schools have become increasingly secularized and democratic. However, in brochures describing the schools to parents of prospective applicants, one does not have to read very deeply between the lines to find at least remnants of the attitudes McLachlan describes. And in headmasters' speeches to alumni, the resemblance is apt to become even more overt. It was precisely to determine if this sort of value-molding environment claimed by prep schools actually does have any effect on the sexual attitudes and behavior of their students that my study was originally designed. This does, indeed, appear to be the case — but not in the way that the schools would applaud.

CHAPTER 7

Sex, Values, and the Prep School Students

"If you are sexually active, you do not belong at this school."

— 20th century headmaster

"For five months in the fall-winter and two in the spring, I had girlfriends living with me in my room."

— Student respondent

In many ways the prep school students and college-bound public school students in my samples were far more similar than dissimilar. This should not be surprising. Whatever differences may exist between the socio-environmental forces impinging on prep school and public school students, there are more than enough other forces to counterbalance them. These forces are undoubtedly part of the one feature that all of the respondents shared: adolescence. In about six years, the respondents in these study groups had undergone the radical physical revolution we label puberty, with all of the emotional stresses it entails. They had begun the psychological trauma of leaving the family nest and moved from a world of general gender segregation to one of almost universal gender integration. Behaviors and attitudes may be more the result of the developmental period through which all adolescents pass than related to geography, type of school, or any other external factors.

If we agree that, for the most part, prep school students are simply normal, healthy adolescents, then we also must admit that part of this normality is the sexual desire stirring even in the very youngest. In the oldest students, this desire is as strong as it will be at any time in their lives. Surely, most thinking adults will agree that this is perfectly natural and normal. If so, then we must ask why so many students and even more faculty from each of the 16 schools in my sample expressed the view that their schools were, as one respondent expressed it, "afraid to confront the issue of sexuality itself." Doubtless, all the schools mean well. However, any yardstick used to measure their success in shaping their students' values must be calibrated by the schools' own standards. First, how successful are they in their efforts to control sexual activity among their students? Second, how healthy is the view of sex and sexuality they are conveying to their students?

My husband and I both remember incredibly uncomfortable chaperoning assignments at Mount Hermon in which the most unnatural behaviors were supposed to be enforced and natural ones suppressed. In the Fall 1995 issue of the school paper, a 1964 Northfield Mount Hermon graduate recalled the days when the school was gender-segregated:

> I remember dances in which teachers would come around and tell you to stop dancing so close. There was one egregious exception, however — Animal Time. After the social event was over, we would walk to the parking lot to wait for the buses to take the girls back to Northfield or the boys back to Mount Hermon. But the buses wouldn't show up for 15 or 20 minutes, leaving you enough time to release your sexual tensions, or at least as much of them as you could release while standing up. Since this was probably the only opportunity for intimate contact you would have all week, you tried to make the most of it. Needless to say, conversation was not at a premium. Unless of course it was your first date; then you felt incredibly awkward, and you were usually reduced to commenting sarcastically about the gross behavior taking place all around you.

School rules controlling male-female interactions of a personal sort came in for a lot of scornful student criticism (as, in fact, they did from many faculty as well):

> They hated PDA (public demonstration of affection). They wouldn't say *NO,* don't do it, but at the same time it was frowned upon in our handbook, and if you did it on campus you kind of got a bad reputation with the faculty.

"PDA" was a term understood on several campuses. A student from another prep school wrote:

> My school's attitude toward sex was very uptight on the part of the administration. We were lectured on "public displays of affection" as the dean of girls put it. We weren't supposed to kiss while strolling or sitting around campus. Walking arm-in-arm was accepted but frowned upon although neither rule was really listened to by the students. They just did it anyway. You could walk into the common room of either dorm I lived in and find a couple making out. That got a little annoying, because if you wanted to go use the common room or watch TV you felt you were intruding, when they shouldn't be doing that in there anyway.

A rule that my husband always maintained was so ludicrous it simply *had* to be apocryphal appeared several times:

> Dorm visitations were a joke. You had to introduce your "friend" to the faculty dorm person, have the light on [and] the door wide open. Also, the faculty member patrolled the rooms in order to check up on you. Some faculty members were more lenient than others, but generally sexual activity was frowned upon. The school didn't want you to "do it" *on the premises.* [italics mine]
>
> ***
>
> It was a repressive school. There was a strict code regarding visitation policy which stipulated certain rights. There were physical criteria that had to be met; door open; one foot on the floor. Now if it was possible to have sexual contact without violating any of these rules, then sexual contact was "allowed" but if any of these rules were violated, then disciplinary measures would be taken.

Reflecting on some current theories regarding the development of certain sexual fetishes, one wonders if there may not be some prep school graduates who can achieve orgasm only with the door open and one foot on the floor!

How successful are such rules in preventing sexual interaction? My study suggests strongly that, concerning adolescent sexual experience before graduation (including "loss of virginity" as well as the range of experiences), prep school students are significantly more sexually active than their college-bound public school counterparts (see Appendix). Ironically, one faculty member admitted as much, though my results suggest that her assumptions about the reason are incorrect: "Sexual activity is greater among boarding students because [the former] are away from home. Day students are still being supervised by their parents."

Kinsey and his colleagues (1948, 1953) reported that premarital sex occurs less among persons from the higher socioeconomic levels than among those from lower levels. This seems not to be the case if my study results are representative. College preparatory school students *are* generally from the higher socioeconomic levels. Yet, in terms of their own premarital sexual behavior, the students in my sample were far more active than their public school counterparts.

Concerning this greater amount of sexual activity reported by the prep school students in my sample, it might be argued that the figures are distorted (to the high side) by the tendency of teenagers, in response to peer pressure, to claim more sexual activity than is actually the case. This certainly is a point to keep in mind in research of this sort. There are several reasons for discounting it as a significant factor here, however. For one, there is no obvious reason to expect that exaggeration of their personal sexual experiences by teenagers would be any higher among prep school students than among their public school counterparts. Thus such exaggeration, even if it did occur, would not be expected to affect any significant differences between the two groups. Furthermore, because the questionnaire was anonymous, it would not be subject to peer review and therefore such bragging would be to no avail. Finally, both in additional written comments and during interviews, several of the college prep students made explicit reference to this tendency to exaggerate on the part of themselves and their peers. This suggests that estimates by the sample student respondents of the actual amount of sexual activity occurring at their schools may well have taken this factor into consideration.

How, then, can we account for the greater sexual activity of prep school students in comparison to their public school counterparts? When one considers the vast amount of time and effort expended by prep schools to prevent sexual activity, these results are surprising. Several faculty members expressed their suspicion that, by making sexual contact such a big "no-no," they might, instead, be making it a big "yes-yes." As one put it:

> Sometimes I wondered how much the "forbidden fruit" aspect of sex caused it to seem more attractive to students who might not otherwise have become sexually active yet. There seemed to be definite peer pressure to break rules.

I think the importance of this observation is considerable. It suggests that the degree to which prep school students are more sexually active than their public school counterparts may, ironically, be attributable to the strenuous efforts of their schools to prevent it. This hypothesis predicts that any success a school may have with some students in preventing sexual expression on campus might lead to a flurry of sexual activity during vacations or weekends when the students have off-campus time. Indeed, some students said as much. This "powder keg" hypothesis is lent some support from my data showing that, despite the fact that preppies spend almost nine months of the year living on campus, the home is the leading area reported for sexual activity, usually the female's home. On campus, if in a residence, sexual activity takes place more often in male dormitories than in female dormitories. From the standpoint of the school, therefore, these demographic factors allow school officials to argue that policing sexual activity is more a parent responsibility than a school responsibility.

Other hypotheses are possible, of course. For example, Kinsey and his colleagues reported that the degree of religious devoutness is a factor in determining the amount of sexual experience; the more devout, the less sexual activity. My sample prep school students labeled themselves as less religious than did the public school students. One might hypothesize that the fewer religious prohibitions against premarital sex might be a factor. Yet the vast majority of both prep school and public school graduates denied believing that God had any interest at all in their sexual behavior.

Another plausible hypothesis is related to the possibility that, far more than public schools, prep schools are mini-versions of the liberal arts college. To the extent that a liberal education is "liberating," in the sense of putting the individual in charge of his or her own values formation and behavior, to that same extent it might have a liberalizing effect on sexual behavior when compared with the more restrictive Western norm. Slight support is given to this hypothesis by noting that it was their educational aims and ambitions (whether the student was college-bound or not) that seemed to account for the differences between my study's total sample and that of Sorensen (see Appendix).

Yet another hypothesis is related to the national or even international flavor of a prep school education as opposed to the rather localized environment of the average public school. A prep school student may have played interscholastic sports with schools in other states and traveled to a foreign country to study its language or carry out an archeological dig. A public school student, on the other hand, tends to be limited to his or her own community and its surrounding areas. Therefore, potential sexual contacts are subject to local mores and customs. As one faculty respondent put it: "Kids or young adults are not influenced as strongly by their school, but rather their surroundings."

Conceivably, the experientially enriched nature of the college preparatory school environment may instill a broader student perspective of life in general, which, in turn, might lead to a richer and more varied sex life. Certainly the students seem to have fun trying to be sexual. At times, the activities seem rather bizarre: "Common type of party was a blow-out party. Candle in the middle — who could put it out." At others, the more standard fare: "After lights [out], the students went to the fields to meet and have sexual intercourse." Another student wrote:

> There was a good deal of sexual activity in my school, especially in my class. I remember things vividly since my first year there (tenth grade) and it got worse as we got older. My best friend (who was also a proctor in our dorm) had her boyfriend in her room (illegally) almost every day. I used to sneak out of the dorm every weekend to go spend the night at my boyfriend's apartment and my senior year (when he no longer had an apartment), I used to sneak him up to my room every weekend and sometimes during the week. It was really easy and lots of kids did it in both the girls' and guys' dorms. It also included everyone from freshmen to seniors (being very few freshmen and very many seniors).

Even those most favored by the faculty fool them at their own game. One female student wrote:

> Students in schools such as [name of school], I think, finally decide it's worth it to take enormous chances involving sex. My junior year, I was a proctor (as well as my senior year), but that year in particular I spent numerous Saturday nights in my boyfriend's dorm room. He graduated *cum laude*, I was an honor student, and we were both well thought of by many faculty members and administrators. All hell would have broken loose if we'd ever been caught, as we were usually breaking more rules by smoking and drinking. However, my thoughts on the subject were that it was important enough for me to be alone with him — a luxury not legally afforded to us at school — and I would take the chance. We were never caught.

It will probably not come as a surprise to many of the prep school faculty among my respondents that I could go on and on listing such incidents provided to me by their students.

One thing comes across clearly. By their restrictive policies on male-female interactions, the schools appear to be fostering precisely the sort of sexual attitudes and behavior that, publicly at least, they most decry. There seems little doubt that many prep schools are conveying to both students and faculty the impression that they view sexuality as if it were some sort of malevolent force to be kept tightly under control until released into the larger confines of traditional marriage, a "sex is dirty — save it for the one you love" philosophy. The result of giving this impression, in combination with rules enacted to limit expression in personal relationships, appears to be a campus sexual atmosphere that is anything but ideal. The statement of a female student put this far more eloquently than I could:

> The faculty . . . tried very hard to halt any attempts made by the students to form "normal" male-female relationships . . . but the problem that arose from this was that a great deal of fear and anxiety grew within us while we did all of this illegally, for fear of getting caught and being humiliated (because most faculty scorned any type of sexual relationship at all). . . . There existed this bit of hypocrisy by the faculty, preaching the importance of male-female relationships . . . yet not allowing for these to ever grow and form, let alone prosper and really develop into good, solid relationships. Thus one-night stands flourished for the most part and long-lasting relationships usually crumbled under the pressure.

This theme of school policy frustrating the formation of healthy relationships was one repeated many times in a variety of ways. A male student commented:

> [Name of school] was a very sexually frustrated place, both faculty and students. Although there was a fair amount of sexual activity, it was generally of the one-night-stand type. Time and negative attitudes of faculty made long-term relationships quite uncommon.

Another wrote:

> There were seven deadly sins at [name of school] and the committing of any of these was grounds for immediate dismissal. Apart from the usual drink, drugs, etc., one of the "taboos" was "unauthorized" visitations but these were structured in such a way as to do more harm than good. . . .

The net result was that intimate relationships were both enticed and frustrated by the semi-privacy, and casual (i.e., nonsexual) male-female relationships were greatly discouraged. . . . After asking permission for visitation a couple of times last year my girlfriend and I would just go over to my dorm, walk up to my room and lock the door. Unfortunately, as I am not really relaxed breaking rules, this often led to a bit of the "quickie in a back alley" feeling and I believe was a serious detriment not only to our sexual relationship (as I am sure it was meant to be) but also to the personal relationship. Overall I would say the school did a very poor job of addressing this issue. Although [it] has been coed for over a decade there remains predominantly a single-sex attitude that is deeply based in the tradition of the school. . . . Best of luck with your research and PLEASE make the results available to the schools!

Besides permitted male-female dormitory visitations (by no means universal in prep schools), prep school social functions involving males and females began with afternoon "tea dances" in the early part of this century, when most schools were gender segregated, and progressed to movie dates, full-fledged dances, and, of course, the traditional prom. One gets the impression that these are tolerated only as a release valve in order to prevent sexual explosions. Such functions always are controlled heavily and well-chaperoned. The artificiality of the situation is not lost on the students. One female student wrote:

[Name of school] and its faculty members completely discouraged any social life for its students. This was its great weakness. Sure we had dances and movies to attend but the social scene and the environment was far too protective and false. The relationship between a boy and a girl was stunted and manipulated simply for the reason that there was nowhere for the couple to go if they wanted any sort of privacy. The relationships, consequently, were frustrating and often felt artificial.

And another female student maintained that:

at Saturday dances, no more than 20 percent of the school
body showed up at the function. Most of the other kids were
either drinking or taking drugs or having sex; some, a combination of two or more of those mentioned. I think that most
of the sexual activities at my school were one-night stands;
sometimes these relationships lasted for a day or two.

Another student noted that there was a lot of "casual sex" at
her school and saw male students as "incredibly uncommunica-
tive, insensitive people, after women for their bodies alone." She
blamed the school for encouraging such views by its placing "a
high social value in being 'cool' and athletic."

It quickly became clear to me that most of the students in my
sample saw their schools as fostering poor values, ironic indeed.
They sensed (correctly, I believe) that the faculty and administrators favored students who were "good looking." The result is to
create, as one female student put it, "an esoteric clan, created sole-
ly on the basis of appearance." What this student (and many others
in my sample) noted were elitist practices on the part of her
school. The attitudes of the sampled students often mirrored those
of their schools in this regard. Concerning pornography, for
example, the amount of reading of pornographic materials was
virtually identical for both prep and public school students. Yet,
while prep school students report reading pornography with significantly less personal guilt than did the public school students,
they would still restrict access to these materials to others. Such
"it's okay for *us* but not for *them*" attitudes, for example, are
reflected by former President George Bush (a Phillips Andover
grad). Bush admitted, when pressed by an interviewer, that he
would support his granddaughter's choice should she elect to have
an abortion. Yet he campaigned against President Clinton in 1992
on a Republican Party platform that sought to outlaw abortion for
all women. Clearly there is a strong element of intellectual elitism;
and as I stressed earlier, prep schools historically have represented
an elitist class. To a considerable degree, they still do.

Another classic example of prep school student elitist thinking
appeared in a 9 October 1993 Kent School student newspaper

article dealing with whether the school should make condoms available to its students. The faculty advisor to the paper made sure his flanks were covered in allowing such a topic to be discussed by noting that "the school's discouragement of sexual activity is a non-negotiable issue" and that "it is highly unlikely that contraceptives will soon be available for school distribution." He then went on to justify the article because the issue of AIDS is "a compelling and relevant adolescent issue and [is] thus appropriate for mature discussion in the NEWS." In the "con" portion of the article, written by a male student, the author admits that Kent students can and do get condoms elsewhere. He then states that "Kent students are smart, they know what the risks are. . . . In inner city schools where condom distribution is a common occurrence, students are not as well informed as we are. They lead a different lifestyle than we do and may need condoms given to them. We know the risks, and most would not allow ourselves to get involved in a game of Russian roulette. We don't need to be given condoms in order to use them." A more compelling example of a "we vs. those others" attitude could hardly be imagined.

Beyond this blatant elitism, the student author's lack of intellectual openness is attested to by the opening of his next paragraph, which reads:

> No matter what anyone says, the distribution of condoms
> encourages sex. At a school where such an emphasis is placed
> on morals and standard of living, it would be hypocritical to
> hand out contraceptives. We are an Episcopal school. Is that
> not enough to silence any supporters of this argument? Maybe
> one could have such a policy at a public school, but never at
> a private Episcopal boarding school like Kent.

The writer of the "pro" portion of the article, a female student, neatly turns aside this religious argument and in so doing provides some food for thought for the faculty advisor and her school. She writes:

> It is almost ironic that one would say that because this is
> a "Christian" school we can not distribute condoms; rather,

it should be said that because Kent is a religious school our first priority is to protect lives, and therefore promote "safe sex."

The prep school students in my sample showed remarkable perception concerning what was actually going on at their schools — far more, it seems, than did the faculty. The sexual activities of one headmaster with both students and faculty were known to the student body weeks before wind of it arrived elsewhere and a quiet resignation could be arranged. Similarly, the students in my sample were quite attuned to goings-on in their school community. One wrote:

> [There was] plenty of extramarital sex going on. [I feel] it is an incestuous community. There are singles sleeping with other faculty and also sleeping with students.

The CBS *60 Minutes* segment dealing with the Choate-Rosemary Hall/Emma Willard School drug bust effectively demonstrated that students are adept at carrying out forbidden practices right under the noses of the administration and faculty. The headmaster could not believe it when told by commentator Ed Bradley that one of his trusted peer counselors had been in on the drug deal: "I think you probably want to check your facts again, you're just not accurate" was the response. They did check their facts and found that actually *two* peer counselors were involved. While this must have been a humiliating experience for the headmaster, he can take comfort in the fact that it could just as well have been any other headmaster or faculty member. Furthermore, if it applies to drugs, it most surely applies to sex. And, as I pointed out previously, at the prep schools in my sample, the two quite often went hand in hand. By treating drug use and sex as comparable offenses, the schools are lumping together in their students' minds that which is unnatural and destructive with that which should be viewed as natural and affirming.

CHAPTER 8

Homosexuality and Values

"In my age, we laughed at queers, fairies, and anyone who was thought to be a homosexual. It was a hideous thing and no one talked about it, much less ever confessed to being a homosexual. Now they are coming out of the closet. . . . That frightens me because when they come out of the closet, they are a much larger group than we expected."

— Reverend Jerry Falwell,
How You Can Help Clean Up America

Faculty questionnaire item: "What would be the reaction of your school to a homosexual faculty member who 'came out of the closet'?"
Response: "So long, faggot!!"

A few years ago, the magazine of one leading New England college preparatory school carried an article extolling the achievements of one of its graduates and former faculty member. Son of one of the school's most respected staff members, star varsity athlete, A+ student, inspiring teacher — the story was a natural for such a publication. The article contained one glaring omission, however. Its author forgot to mention or, more likely, came to the school too late to learn one pertinent bit of information. The featured graduate had been dismissed from the faculty when it came to the school's attention that he was gay.

There is a long history of this sort of action at independent schools. In 1872 a very famous and talented teacher at England's Eton abruptly left the school. While no official explanation was ever forthcoming, the discovery of some letters disclosed his homosexuality. An outstanding scholar, the teacher had authored a textbook used at Eton. Though it continued to be used for the next 80 years, his name was removed from the book. In his book, *The Old School Tie*, Jonathan Gathorne-Hardy describes the aftermath of the incident as follows:

> There descended one of those profound and mysterious silences which public schools, like the families they all to some extent are, let fall to protect those who belong to them. (1977, p. 188)*

Anyone who has taught in a prep school is familiar with such silences. Such behavior is symptomatic of the intense paranoia that infects prep schools whenever an issue arises that they perceive as a threat to their image. In no case is this more evident than in the case of homosexuality. By virtue of being officially denied, it is therefore unofficially acknowledged through rumor and innuendo. In my experience, most prep school faculty and administrators remain almost childishly afraid to confront the issue. They thereby open the door to those whose insecurity with their own sexuality leads them to establish a cruelly repressive atmosphere in which both students and faculty become victimized. Male faculty are often the perpetrators by idolizing the male "jock" who, it is assumed, must be heterosexual. The female "jock" faculty member or student athlete, on the other hand, is suspect and often subjected to cruel or insensitive locker room talk and bathroom graffiti.

The amount of homosexual orientation reported by my student sample (about 10%) squares with the results of Sorensen and Hass. Sorensen reported somewhat less than 10%, Hass some-

---

*In England, the "public" schools are the equivalent to our private schools.

what more.* The age of first homosexual experience reported by Sorensen was between 11 and 12 years of age for males and between six and 10 years of age for females. My results were in agreement with these data, though the prep school males in my sample reported a lower age (between five and eight years) of first homosexual experience than did my male public school respondents (between 10 and 12 years). Of course, same-sex sexual interaction between children of these ages is not an indicator as to whether these children actually identify as homosexual.

There were no significant differences in the amount of actual homosexual behavior among prep school and public school males. The finding by Hass that more teenage females than males were open to same-sex sexual experiences in the future is also in line with my data. He also found that the females in his sample were more tolerant of homosexual behavior in others than they were for themselves. This, too, was borne out in my study and that of Sorenson. Only in the attitude of the prep school male were my findings and others reversed: Prep school males were significantly more homophobic than were public school males.

It is possible that the significantly higher degree of homophobia shown by prep school males is related to the strong homosexual overtones associated with all-male prep schools or dormitories. One has only to read male dormitory bathroom graffiti or listen to male students and faculty to note considerable fear and nervousness about this matter, though coeducation has gone a long way toward establishing a healthier and more mature viewpoint. Fear of being labeled "homosexual" in a society where bigotry against gays abounds often leads people to publicly express

---

*The research data of Robert Sorensen and Aaron Hass on adolescent sexuality pertinent to my study, as well as those of Kinsey et al., are provided in the Appendix. The recent issue of gays in the military has led to a questioning of the Kinsey team's introduction of the approximately 10% figure, with the suggestion that a more accurate figure is actually between 1% to 3%. I believe much of the confusion relates to a misunderstanding of the Kinsey team's work and their conclusions. Of course, for the issue of civil rights for gays and lesbians, a precise number, even if it were possible to obtain one, is irrelevant.

homophobic attitudes designed to convince others of their heterosexuality or to mask homosexual leanings they dare not admit.

Historian Michael Goodich (1977) has pointed out that the
pogroms carried out by the Church against homosexuals in the
Middle Ages were often the result of widespread homosexual
activity within the clergy. Similarly, fear of being labeled homosexual in a society where bigotry against gays abounds often
leads to publicly expressed homophobic attitudes designed to
convince others of their heterosexuality or to mask homosexual
leanings they dare not admit. Sidney Blumenthal (1997), writing
about Whittaker Chambers, whose testimony to the Senator
Joseph McCarthy hearings in the 1950s helped send Alger Hiss
to jail and launch the political career of Richard M. Nixon, suggests that, with the demise of Communism, the "enemy within"
has been replaced in the mind of the political right by the "homosexual menace." He further notes that right-wing conservative
groups have often served as "the ultimate closet" for homosexuals, citing as examples the late FBI director J. Edgar Hoover,
McCarthy hearings legal council Roy Cohn, and Francis Cardinal
Spellman, archbishop of New York. The revelation a few years
ago (through their arrest for solicitation of minors) of the homosexuality of two United States congressmen who had campaigned
against civil rights for homosexuals provides perhaps yet another
example of this phenomenon, as may the more recent coming out
of the closet by the Reverend Mel White, the ghost biographer of
evangelists Jim Bakker, Billy Graham, Jerry Falwell, D. James
Kennedy, and Pat Robertson and long a staunch supporter of the
Religious Right's campaign against gay rights.* At least one the-
ologian-historian has suggested a similar explanation concerning St.
Paul, whose fulminations against same-sex sexual interactions have
provided grist for the hate mills of some contemporary evangelists.

---

*At an April 2000 conference on Gay and Lesbian Civil Rights held in
Charlottesville, Virginia, at which they were both invited speakers, Reverend
White informed my husband that he had also been scheduled to write a biography of Oliver North but that White's coming out of the closet quickly can-
celled that idea.

All-male or all-female institutions, including prep schools, often exhibit both a higher incidence of homosexuality than found in the general population and seemingly also a greater fear of it. The accepted practice of "fagging" in British public schools, in which a younger pupil must perform certain services for an upperclassman, had obvious homosexual as well as sado-masochistic overtones. Like the extramarital affairs of British royalty, however, such matters were not admitted publicly and their true nature never discussed. If, as prep school historian J. McLachlan and others have maintained, school athletics provides a substitute for sex, they have no less been used as an affirmation of "manliness" by both faculty and students — such "manliness" providing convincing "evidence" of heterosexuality. One student in my sample recalled being hurried with some friends to the athletic fields by their coach with: "Come on you guys, what are you, a bunch of fairies?" To the credit of these students, my respondent reported that most were shocked at this blatant display of bigotry. Unfortunately, several of my student and faculty respondents indicated that the attitudes reflected in the coach's comment often are found among both prep school students and faculty.

Faculty responses were mixed to the question heading this chapter, "What would be the reaction of your school to a homosexual faculty member who 'came out of closet'?" Their general drift is probably best conveyed by quoting a few representative responses, with only slight attempts to categorize. The negative view produced the following:

> Faculty member would be forced to leave.
>
> ***
>
> Disapproval at best.
>
> ***
>
> Shock and disapproval.
>
> ***
>
> Surprise and horror.
>
> ***
>
> The board of trustees and the headmaster would probably request the resignation of the faculty member.

**

Not sure — probably the school would try to have the individual resign.

**

Shocked. He would be encouraged to leave the boarding school or *get out of the dorm.* [emphasis added]

The last comment reflects the widely accepted myth of the prowling, victim-seeking homosexual, posing the threat of sexual exploitation of the students under his or her care. Statistically, of course, it is heterosexuals, not homosexuals, who pose the greater threat.

A few saw the situation differently, depending on the sex of the individual. For example: "A male faculty member would be fired. If a female was in the same situation, our administration would turn its head and pretend the situation did not exist."

The suggestion that the school administration might not deal with such a case totally above board and, in fact, might be more concerned with appearance than substance was a discouragingly common theme:

Tough to predict. The school has invited homosexuals to talk to students, but it might not be so liberal to its own faculty.

**

Probably okay, in a knee-jerk liberal way, as long as the homosexuality was an abstraction that didn't directly affect the community.

**

No reaction *unless it was evident to the students.* [emphasis added]

**

This is not an issue our school has had to face. I think it would be liberal, but again appearances seem important. No doubt most people would wish he'd "stayed in" [the closet].

**

Tough to gauge, but probably "good-bye" *due to "image consciousness" and "role model" concepts.* [emphasis added]

***

> He would be advised to be more discreet or. . . I hate to
> say it. . . to leave — I think the school would tolerate it as
> long as he or she did not become a gay rights activist.

This last one is a shocker. One can imagine the reaction if a member of any other minority group were told, "Yes, you can be on our faculty, but don't try to work for the civil rights of others of your kind." Yet there is evidence that this respondent is correct. A 1986 Associated Press article in the *San Juan Star* reported that the Horace-Mann-Bernard School refused to print biographical material in its alumni magazine concerning the civil rights activity on behalf of gays by two of its graduates, one a professor of history at Lehman College.

The real bombshell in the survey, however, came from the respondent who wrote:

> He would be fired. At [name of school] each faculty
> member is asked seven questions before he/she is hired. The
> questions are probably illegal. Are you homosexual? Do you
> carry outstanding debts? Do you have a problem with drugs,
> alcohol, etc.? Some have found the first question offensive.
> A woman from [name of another school] was so mad when
> she was asked if she was homosexual that she left the inter-
> view.

The respondent did not indicate whether the woman was offended because of the possibility of someone thinking she might be a lesbian or because of the bigotry implicit in the question or its gross violation of her individual right to personal privacy.

When I first received the returned questionnaires from my faculty respondents, I merely scanned them before filing them for later analysis. It was not until I was able to place all the answers to each question in groups that I felt the full effect of what they were saying. As I already noted, most faculty responses were negative to the question concerning how their school would probably handle the discovery of an openly gay faculty member. It is

significant, however, that each respondent put considerable distance between his or her own position and that of the school. With
only four exceptions, faculty members' perceptions of the
response of their colleagues or their schools' administration to an
out-of-the-closet gay faculty member were hardly different than
one would expect to find at any highly conservative institution.
But the responses of most faculty members also showed clearly
that they were ashamed of their schools' attitudes toward gays.

It is easy to see why they would feel this way. After all, we are
dealing with some of the finest college preparatory schools in the
country. It is difficult in reading these comments to see much of
the respect for individuality, fairness, tolerance, or compassion
generally associated with the Judeo-Christian tradition often
championed by these schools. In this and several other issues
dealt with in my survey, it is the faculty, not just the students, who
perceive their schools as being, at best, hypocritical; at worst,
bigoted and intellectually dishonest.

As discouraging as these results may be, the fact that most faculty respondents felt alone in possessing a more knowledgeable
and humane approach to an understanding of homosexuality
(and, indeed, sexuality in general) gives considerable ground for
hope. True, there were one or two faculty members who still
viewed homosexuals as threats to the students. There was even
one who, while he would turn over students caught in heterosexual intercourse to the dean for disciplinary action, would turn
over students caught in homosexual interaction to "the medical
staff." On the whole, however, the self-described responses of the
faculty members of their own personal reaction on discovering
two students engaged in same-sex sexual interaction, in contrast
to what they perceived would be those of their colleagues, were
tolerant and supportive. Typical comments of this sort included:

> Leave them alone for a while, and then would go out of
> my way to talk to one or both in an affirming way to coun-
> teract the many negative reactions they probably got or
> would expect. I would encourage them to seek out a gay
> support group.

***

If I knew the students well enough, I would talk to them individually to be sure they were feeling good about themselves and their decision.

***

Initiate a counseling session and carry conversation and referral (to a dean or counselor) only as far as student seems to want and need (e.g., question: Does this relationship feel nurturing or exploitative?).

***

I would try to protect the students from the homophobic outrage (real or manufactured) in the school community.

It would be difficult to find fault with such nonjudgmental, supportive counseling. Equally refreshing was the honestly expressed acknowledgment by many faculty of their own homophobia. Several seemed anxious to deal with it. One respondent wrote:

I really don't know. I suppose I am no more or less immune than anyone else to the tendency to be bigoted against homosexuals, which I view as the result of the need in our society to suppress someone. It used to be blacks, then women, now it's gays. Most certainly this school is intolerant in this regard, but I suppose most are.

My anonymous survey questionnaire did not ask the faculty respondents to identify their sexual orientation. There is no reason, however, to suspect that the figures have changed very much from data gathered by other researchers in such institutions in the past. It is interesting, however, that student perceptions of the percent of gay faculty ranged considerably higher than faculty estimates. Indeed, one married faculty couple informed me in no uncertain terms that there were *no* gay men or lesbians at their school. Yet, at this same school, a female faculty member informed me that she recalled "meeting one married faculty member at a gay bar dance. He was shocked at being discovered but was able to talk about it later. I did not blow his cover." A similar story of the discovery of a faculty member by a student at a "safe" gay bar (one where his identity would not be revealed) was related at another school.

Student prejudices concerning homosexuals mirrored that of their schools. Those who were gay or lesbian themselves understandably found it expedient to remain well in the closet. Students also were aware that their schools would not knowingly hire a homosexual.

Several students noted that, as one put it, "the school encourages homosexuality unconsciously." He made it clear he meant that the school's restrictive policies on heterosexual social interaction left homosexual contacts one of the few remaining options. Gathorne-Hardy suggests in his book, *The Old School Tie*, that such schools may actually do their homosexual students a favor by providing an atmosphere in which they can discover their homosexual orientation early. Writer Robert Graves noted in a description of his school days at Charterhouse, "for every one born homo-sexual there are at least ten permanent pseudo-homosexuals created by the public school system"(1929, p. 29).* This concept of restrictive heterosexual contacts opening the door for homosexual outlets is similar to what Kinsey and his colleagues reported for their interviewees who, for religious reasons, were strongly prohibited from social contact with persons of the opposite sex as adolescents: a rise in same-sex sexual contacts.

More serious, however, were the comments of several students on the use of homophobia to wield political power. One wrote:

> Amongst the student body, there was a prejudice against homosexuality and occasionally rumors that so-and-so was homosexual or lesbian. Sometimes the prejudice would be used politically against someone running for a school office, by circulating rumors of [the candidate] being homosexual.

---

*Such "situational homosexuality" is quite different from "constitutional" homosexuality. It is similar to homosexual acts that occur in prisons; once released, the former inmates return to their regular heterosexual orientation if that is what it was when they entered.

A better example of the use of sexual bigotry for wielding power could hardly be found. Yet, given the attitudes of their schools toward homosexuality as perceived by both students and faculty, it is difficult to see how matters could be any different.

Reflecting on his own interview-based research concerning homosexuality, Alfred Kinsey suggested that the heterosexual-homosexual world should not be divided into "sheep and goats." The first of the Kinsey studies appeared in 1948. The country was shocked to read that 37% of red-blooded, Midwestern American males had at least some overt same-sex sexual experience to the point of orgasm between adolescence and old age. Fifty percent of those who remained single until age 35 had done so. Eighteen percent were bisexual, in other words, had as much homosexual as heterosexual experience. Thirteen percent reported having had sufficient homosexual experience between the ages of 15 and 55 to have been classified as gay. The numbers were lower among women but followed the same pattern. As a result of these and other of the Kinsey research team's findings, Kinsey developed a 0–6 scale of sexual orientation, ranging from exclusively hetero-sexual to exclusively homosexual, with the majority of the popu-lation in the study somewhere in between. It is important to note that this does not mean that individuals anywhere on the scale necessarily act on their sexual preferences. In the case of homo-sexuals especially, intense pressure to conform to the norms of the community undoubtedly serves to suppress their sexual expression. Doubtless fear of loss of job, denial of housing, and social or religious condemnation also are powerful deterrents.

The Kinsey scale is useful in that it describes far more accurate-ly what other research has revealed about human sexual behavior than does the old "sheep and goats" view. Beyond that, it shows how ludicrous discrimination against gays and lesbians actually is: How gay or lesbian must one be in order to be a "goat"?

One is reminded of a law once on the books in a Southern state making anyone who was 1/64 black legally black. The late Dr. Evelyn Hooker's classic blind study of 30 male homosexuals revealed that, by any objective criteria besides their sexual orientation, these men would have been classified as perfectly normal. Such research eventually led to removal of homosexuality from the list of pathological illnesses by the American Psychiatric Association in 1973. That it was on the list at all is a testimonial to the way that so-called medical science has often reinforced prevailing social prejudices and religious views. Anyone inclined to doubt this need only read portrayals of blacks in 19th and early 20th century medical journals as being less intelligent because of a presumed (and incorrect) lower cranial capacity. Similarly, women were portrayed as creatures subject to "hysteria," a condition correctable, of course, by hysterectomies. Paralleling such medical views of blacks and women were theological ones. Blacks were the descendants of Ham, the son who mocked his father Noah's nakedness, and were therefore meant by God to be servants to others. For centuries, the "Ham hypothesis" was used to justify slavery and, despite a 1992 apology, it still remains prevalent in the Dutch Reformed Church, the largest Christian denomination among South African whites. It was not until 1979 that the Church of Jesus Christ of Latter-Day Saints (Mormon) decreed blacks no longer unworthy of their ministry and, despite many converts in Africa, the Church seems still divided on the issue. In the case of women, as the introducers of sin into the world through Eve, all women were tainted; as St. Thomas Aquinas put it, "by their nature" inferior to men and meant to remain in a "state of subjection" (*quia mulier est in status subjectionis*). (In 1978, the Vatican used Aquinas's arguments to reaffirm the denial of the priesthood to women.)

Such examples should serve to remind us that the current climate of fundamentalist Bible thumping against homosexuals simply means that they are merely the most recent target of theological ire. While Western society has at least progressed beyond the point of assigning life imprisonment, torture, or burning at the stake for homosexuals, even in today's supposedly enlightened society they all too often are denied basic civil rights. One could hardly find a better example of the danger of inexorably linking through civil law the formation of our value systems with our Judeo-Christian heritage, for it was medieval Europe's Church-

State union that allowed such atrocities to occur. It is far better to secularize non-repressive values. So doing allows those within religious traditions, as well as those without, to join together in fostering those attributes that surely those in either camp should share: compassion for those who have, and still are, suffering such indignities. As educators, unless there is clear evidence of social pathology, we must also promote tolerance and acceptance of human beings for the sexual persons they *are*, rather than how some think they *should* be.

Still, the old mentality dies hard. One headmaster wrote: "sex educators do surveys on the peculiar theory that if we know what they actually do in such matters we may find out what they *ought* to do." It is, of course, sex researchers, not educators, who do "surveys"; and their data, like those of all sciences, are, of necessity, nonjudgmental. Such "ought to" statements reflect an all-too-common misunderstanding by the public of science and its limitations.

In their college biology textbook, *Biological Science* (W.W. Norton 1986), the late Cornell University biologist William T. Keeton and his co-author James Gould note quite correctly that:

> science . . . cannot make value judgments: it cannot say, for example, that a painting or a sunset is beautiful. And science cannot make moral judgments: it cannot say that war is immoral. It cannot even say that a river should not be polluted. Science can, however, analyze responses to a painting; it can analyze the biological, social, and cultural implications of war; and it can demonstrate the consequences of pollution. It can, in short, try to predict what people will consider beautiful or moral, and it can provide them with information that may help them make value judgments about war or pollution. But the act of making judgments itself is not science.

In the context of homosexuality, such seemingly benign "ought to" statements as that of the above-quoted headmaster are often far from that. It is just this sort of "ought to" or, rather, for homosexuals, "ought *not* to" thinking that has led to their being subjected to (or, worse, feel sufficiently threatened to even volunteer for) "aversive therapy." Such "conversion" therapy has even involved vomiting-inducing drugs or painful electric shock to force homosexuals to become what society thinks they "ought" to be. This "ought," of course, is heterosexual, or, as those whose sexual lives lie on the "ought" rather than "ought not" side of the tracks often label it, "straight" (suggesting strongly that those who are homosexual are somehow crooked). In the light of such benign brutality, Theodore Sizer's association of our Judeo-Christian heritage with "tolerance, compassion, and individualism, etc.," seems far removed from reality.

With such moralistic and judgmental thinking around, the picture revealed concerning homosexuality and the prep school is not an encouraging one. Rather than projecting an image of open-mindedness, tolerance, compassion, and decency, the schools appear to be providing a role model for their students of pretending to be all these yet, in actuality, being the reverse of each. This being the case, it is little wonder that many of their students become cynical about their schools' actions and motives. Lest any of my readers are inclined to discount much of this because they are "just students," I stress again that the worst condemnation of the schools in this matter came from their own faculty.

Oddly, for the beleaguered gay and lesbian community, dealing with the Religious Right is often easier than it is with those whose attitudes seem benevolent. With the former, at least, their "love the sinner, hate the sin" bigotry is clear.* For example, headmaster John Rae's attitude seems remarkably open and tolerant:

---

*Michelle Cottle (*New Republic*, 20 May 1999) reports on the activities of Reverend D. James Kennedy of the Coral Ridge Presbyterian Church in Fort Lauderdale, Florida, showing that this thinking is still alive and well. Kennedy's motto for the "conversion" of homosexuals to heterosexuals states, "It's not about hate. It's about hope." He has been able to finance full-page ads in newspapers across the country. Among the persons for whom Kennedy has provided a platform are George Grant, fond of pointing to the Bible's call for the death penalty for homosexuals, and Gary North, who, according to Cottle, has enumerated the benefits of public stoning: It is cheap, requires no special equipment, and calls for community participation! It should be noted that Kennedy is a minister in the Presbyterian Church in America, an ultra-conservative splinter group that is not part of the Presbyterian Church (USA).

> That many good teachers of both sexes are sublimated homosexuals no one would seriously question. Indeed, their sexual orientation is one reason why they are such good teachers, particularly in their devotion to their pupils. Nor do I think it is remotely true that such teachers inevitably disorientate the sexual interests of their students. (1987, p. 149)

Rae further suggests that Kinsey's scale of sexual orientation is correct and notes that "to talk of exclusive classifications is misleading." He writes:

> There is homosexuality in all of us, and understanding that ought to make us less prejudiced, even though our predominant interest is heterosexual. I have little doubt that the almost hysterical prejudice with which housemasters and headmasters used to respond to the first hint of homosexuality among their pupils was caused by their inability to come to terms with the homosexual elements in their own make–up. (p. 197)

Curiously (and regrettably, I think), Rae seems to discard his own informed viewpoint when he states:

> Should the school teach that a homosexual relationship has equal validity with a heterosexual one? I do not think it should. A school should teach tolerance and understanding but "equal validity" implies that a homosexual relationship is as normal as a heterosexual one and by no twist of logic or semantics can homosexuality be described as normal. It is natural for those involved because it arises from their nature but it is not normal either in terms of statistics or in terms of biological imperative to propagate the species. It cannot be said to have the same validity, the same worth as a heterosexual relationship. To teach children that is to correct prejudice with a lie. (p. 198)

Here, "normal" for Rae appears to be the sexual orientation of the statistical majority, an argument that runs into considerable difficulty when applied elsewhere. He comes down squarely on the nature side of the nature versus nurture debate concerning the "causes" of homosexuality, seemingly unaware that few if any modern developmental biologists pay attention to such either/or arguments. Tying sexual normality to propagation is a theological, rather than biological, argument; nonpropagative sexual interactions are known across the board in nature. Thus, even from Rae's enlightened viewpoint, theological arguments formed centuries before the rise of modern science still sustain and lend "moral" credence to the prejudices with which homosexuals must deal every day.

There is one way in which the issue of homosexuality is a difficult one in our society. As one civil libertarian noted, it is easy for a white male to march in a black civil rights march or in one for ratification of the Equal Rights Amendment. No one will mistake him for a member of the disadvantaged minority. This is not the case if one marches in a gay rights parade: The person who does so is subject to precisely the same bigotry he or she had the courage to demonstrate against, with all the social and financial risks that this entails. Perhaps even more tragic is the comment made by a black man to a gay man on this same risky matter — marching for their civil rights — that at least blacks had the support of their families and churches, while gays and lesbians often ended up being rejected by both.

Prep school students are still at an age when their value systems are forming. Therefore education concerning these matters is an area in which their schools could take an active leadership role. From my faculty respondents' perceptions of their institution, such a hope may be groundless. But I believe that there are reasons for being optimistic. In its Spring 1991 *Bulletin*, Phillips Academy, Andover, published an interview with poet Paul Monette (Class of 1963), who spoke with an Andover English teacher. Much of what Monette had to say was hardly complimentary:

> I feel an enormous amount of bitterness about both my high school and college years. I can't even measure my adolescent years because it's as if I didn't exist during those years. The closet is a place where you do not exist. To recall that period is to chronicle lost time. There's a kind of an

amnesia of pain. Andover was a place that was deeply straight and status quo and deeply macho. No shadow of homosexuality was ever mentioned in four years, not even in courses like ancient history.

But it was clear that some healing also had taken place:

> Happily, my return to Andover for five summers to teach in the Summer Session gave me a new admiration and affection for some of the people I felt distanced from as a student. Working with. . . faculty as colleagues and equals was a good growing experience, and coeducation was thrilling after the idiocy of eight years of non-coeducation at Andover and Yale. . . . I was so pleased to hear of the Gay/Straight Alliance at Andover. It's reassuring to know the issue has finally been raised, that it's part of the school's consciousness. Otherwise, tremendous isolation would mark every gay and lesbian person's experience of Phillips Academy.

A later article in another Phillips Andover *Bulletin* notes that 30% of teenage suicides are related to anguish about sexual orientation and states that Andover teachers today "realize the humane need to educate all members of the community in order to accord justice and respect to all teachers, staff and students" (Edmonds 1995).

Equally encouraging is the generally open manner in which Phillips Exeter handled the arrest and later conviction of a former, presumably gay, faculty member for allegedly involving his students in child pornography and the "peeping Tom" videos made without the students' knowledge. The school's statement in its Spring 1993 *Bulletin* properly noted that the teacher's behavior "violated the trust inherent in the student-teacher relationship," labeling such behavior as "inexcusable and wrong." Note that the stress was on the exploitative nature of the acts, rather than the teacher's sexual orientation.

Equally encouraging was the evolution of attitudes shown in the letters to the editor section of the same issue of the *Bulletin*. A 1930s Exeter alumnus wrote scornfully of the permissive atmosphere of the school. No longer a hair shirt, it's a wimp. Sensitive, caring, compassionate, they don't describe the PEA I knew. Perhaps the times have passed me by and I should tolerate clubs for homosexuals and lesbians in the name of openness. In the name of decency, I find it revolting.

A 1932 alumnus refers to a "tinge of slime" on the school's hands. Yet four 1987 graduates wrote:

> As former advisees and students of [name of faculty member], we followed with shock and dismay the accusations against him, as well as his trial. Although we hope and believe that [he] is innocent of any actions that would harm another, the purpose of this letter is neither to excuse nor defend him with regard to these allegations. Rather, we would like to comfort and reassure parents of any former or present student who may have been in contact with [name of faculty member] during their years at Exeter. We all lived in a dorm and took classes with [name of faculty member] and have nothing but positive memories and warmest regards for him. He was then, as he is now, a fine educator and friend to us all. He was always there to help and support us through what was, at times, a very tough academic and social environment. For this we are only a few of the many students who are forever grateful to him for being such a positive influence in our lives.

Finally, it should be noted that at least two schools in my sample, Phillips Andover and Hotchkiss, have added sexual orientation to their lists of nondiscrimination criteria concerning prospective students. There may well be more schools that already have followed, or soon will follow, the same ethical path. I read recently a chapter in a book written by an out-of-the-closet lesbian in which she writes of teaching in the "open-mindedness of Northfield Mt. Hermon School" (Greenbaum 1996, p. 85). From my own experience teaching there from 1955 to 1962, this does not surprise me, for it is a truly wonderful college preparatory school and I still treasure warm memories of my former students and faculty colleagues there, both living and deceased. When one considers the history of the Northfield Mount Hermon School's founding, this woman's experience there is as encouraging a sign for the future of tolerance and nonjudgmental acceptance of gay men and lesbians in college preparatory schools as one could possibly imagine.

CHAPTER 9

Gender and Values

"The male faculty is incredibly sexist, but it is less evident because the women here (with notable exceptions) don't know it [sexism] when they see it."
— Female faculty respondent

There probably has been no greater instigator of change in college preparatory schools than in the move of many to become coeducational. This move is now generally (but by no means entirely) viewed as a highly positive one in terms of keeping the schools in tune with a rapidly changing outside world. Writing about the benefits of coeducation (now for more than a quarter-century) at Phillips Exeter Academy, two 1995 graduates reinforce this concept:

The presence of a diverse student body necessitates a broad-based curriculum, one that incorporates the contributions of many different authors and cultures. One only has to look through the Courses of Instruction booklet to see how the curriculum has changed to include gender issues. Sample courses include "Exploring the Voices of Women Writers" and "Toward Equality: Women in Western Society." No longer do English classes read only the poetry of white Anglo-Saxon males, nor is history the study only of prominent men. Uppers study the women of colonial America and seniors read Toni Morrison and Alice Walker. It is this wide range of material that opens our eyes to the issues we will confront in our future. Were there any less diversity at the Academy, many of these issues would never be raised. (Turner and Vorkink 1995, p. 7)

However, it may well be that the suggested benefits of coeducation are greater for formerly all-male schools than for all-female schools. Males still largely control the economic and political reins of our society, and so a strong case can be made for the intellectual development of young women in an environment where their ideas are given equal validity. Writing in the *New York Times* Op-Ed page, former Miss Porter's School head Rachel Belash writes:

> A colleague of mine described a vignette in her all-girls kindergarten class: A small girl surveyed the room, arms akimbo, and sized up the situation. "Thank heavens," she said: " No boys in the block corner." No, there aren't. She won't have to elbow her way to the computer terminals or perhaps feel out of place spending extra time in the physics lab. Her voice will be heard in class, her opinion sought — on every topic — and taken seriously. Whatever the athletic facilities, they are for her alone. Moreover, leadership roles are more available: Girls get experience in managing radio stations, editing student newspapers and literary magazines, heading the debate and mathematics teams — all without having to fight for a place in the sun. Since failure is less threatening, risk-taking becomes more bearable. (1988, p. A19)

Like Miss Porter's, the all-female Emma Willard School was founded in the early 19th century by a woman whose view of women's roles was clearly more in tune with that century. Yet many of its graduates, ranging from Elizabeth Cady Stanton (Class of 1832, from The Troy Female Seminary, as the school was then known) and Jane Fonda (1955) were hardly models of non-assertiveness. As Fonda herself noted in the Spring 1986 *Emma Willard Bulletin*:

> There's a lot to be said for being in an all-woman environment. It's perhaps the only time in a young woman's life that she can be exposed to the best and the brightest of her own sex.

Accepted by some all-male schools, coeducation was resisted angrily by others. When the Hotchkiss School decided to become coeducational in the 1970s, one alumnus, Class of 1915, saw it in clearly sexual terms: "Ho! Ho! Ho! Hotchkiss hasn't the money to build a maternity hospital large enough." Another, Class of 1932, wrote in the Fall 1994 *Hotchkiss Magazine*:

> Not believing in coeducation in boarding schools, I am writing to you what I wrote to Princeton: when coeducation begins, my contributions end. Let the girls' parents pay. How can a master throw chalk at girls? The math problems would have to use diapers instead of bombs, canoes, and Goering & Mussolini on motorcycles. Most unseemly.

One older male prep school faculty member, who granted me a privately taped interview at his school, described the atmosphere:

> [There was] bitter resentment over the merger of the girls' school with the boys'. There was security in having the school all-male. In the beginning there were no female administrators, now there are both. At the time there were violent arguments — many wanted the school to be a boys' school forever. Some still feel that way.

Interestingly, this interviewee said he noted that most of this resentment came from male faculty who were themselves brought up in all-male prep schools. While unwilling to express his own feelings on the matter, he implied that this was less of a problem for him since he had gone to coeducational public schools.

At some schools, cruel and dehumanizing incidents followed coeducation. A few male teachers who had vehemently opposed it often took out their frustrations by harassing female students in their classes, either by ridiculing their errors or subjecting them to biting sarcasm. In other cases, far more common, the wrongs were simply in the form of unintentional insensitive remarks. Unfortunately, there seems to have been a lack of administrative sensitivity and leadership to deal with such matters. One school head reviewer of an early draft of this chapter wrote of being shocked at the "old boy network" mentality of the school head population when she first entered the independent school world in the late 1980s. She went on to describe her impression of:

> an absolute lack of sophistication and understanding relative to gender issues. With more feminist heads (both women and men) coming onto the scene, there is hope — but [in my view] the attitudes you describe are still deeply entrenched.

A few college preparatory schools have been coed from the start (for example, Cushing Academy). Most, however, began as either all-male or all-female, a sort of "separate-but-equal" (though they were hardly the latter) philosophy reminiscent of the racially segregated schools of the South. Because the male institution was usually better equipped, achievement of coeducation usually meant that it was the young women who moved. For example, Abbot Academy in Andover, Massachusetts, seemed lost in the enveloping folds of the neighboring Phillips Academy, Andover, and the Chaffee School for Girls vacated its home of 46 years to move to the all-male Loomis campus to become the Loomis Chaffee School. Of the 16 schools involved in my study, only Concord Academy was an all-female school that, after admitting male students, remained where it was and, according to one of my female school head correspondents, managed to "retain its original values and ethos." In the union of the Mount Hermon School for Boys and the Northfield School for Girls to form the coeducational Northfield Mount Hermon, both schools possessed magnificent campuses and facilities, and thus coeducation was achieved by some students of either sex moving from one campus to the other.* This is not to imply, however, that all the facilities for males and females were given equal consideration before their merger. For example, when it came to deciding which school would receive a new gymnasium, it was hardly a

---

*Evangelist founder Dwight L. Moody had made certain that the schools were separated by a five-mile distance. Possibly he felt that this distance, with the icy cold Connecticut River in between, would be more than sufficient to cool the ardor of any lusty young man who might feel inclined to sneak over to the female campus. Moody probably could never have conceived of the reverse.

matter for discussion. Though the old gymnasium at Mount Hermon was far superior to the one at Northfield, Mount Hermon got the new facility.

My first college preparatory school teaching experience was at the always coeducational Cushing Academy. My second and third appointments were at the Mount Hermon School for Boys and the Northfield School for Girls before the schools were merged. My fourth appointment, at Loomis Chaffee, occurred two years after the first female students were admitted in 1970. Therefore, I did not experience directly what some of my colleagues referred to as a "difficult transitional period" in the history of their school. I did, however, witness the attempts of the administration to deal with such problems as those posed by male teachers, who had taught only males for years, trying to cope with female students for the first time.

Few schools seem to have anticipated the need for any sort of faculty or staff preparation for the entry of female students into all-male campus domains. It was assumed that everything would take care of itself. Most certainly, I had not anticipated any problems, though, along with most of my female faculty and staff colleagues, I was well aware of the often rampant sexism on prep school campuses. In response to such problems as the ones cited previously, and while I was still teaching at Loomis Chaffee, then headmaster Frederick G. Torrey arranged a session for the faculty with a psychologist trained in dealing with gender relationship problems. Just how much good this session accomplished is difficult to say. Most certainly it was an eye-opener for me, my husband (spouses were encouraged to attend), and others.

The psychologist illustrated his points with "games." I am not generally at ease with such an approach, but in this case the effects were most revealing. Game one involved putting on the standard lapel name tags, but with the women using their maiden names and the men adopting their wives' maiden names rather than their own. Considering the innocuous nature of the task, the effects were electric. There was much nervous laughter and giggling on the part of both sexes. One man joked that he couldn't remember his wife's maiden name. Two or three men simply refused to do it, with at least one man's wife supporting him. I had often read in feminist literature about the power of names and the loss of power a name change often symbolizes. The reactions to the name-tag game drove home the point to a degree that nothing else could even have approached.

The second game involved voting for another role reversal, a Miss America-type bathing beauty contest, with the men as contestants and the women as judges. From my knowledge of prep school faculty in general, as well as the reaction to the name-tag game in particular, it was obvious that this game was never going to get off the ground. It was not needed, however. The psychologist's main goal was attained in the ensuing discussion. When asked why she voted against the game, one woman faculty member stated, "I could not put my husband through such humiliation." However, few of the men in the audience seemed to see anything wrong with women being displayed in this way and neither did some of the women.

The last exercise was designed to illustrate how the separation of sexes may lead to the viewing of women as sexual objects in ways that are both exploitative and degrading. The exercise involved sending a male faculty member to the bathroom of a male dormitory and faithfully copying down the graffiti on the walls. (The meeting was held at a time when the students were off campus but before the graffiti could be painted over, as it is during each vacation.) While this was being done, the psychologist made some predictions about the violent and sexually exploitative nature of the graffiti that would be found, noting that this sort of graffiti is especially prevalent in all-male institutions. He also commented on the tendency of all-male societies to glorify competition and the use of violence as a means of settling disputes.

The faculty member returned and the graffiti was read to us. It was exceedingly disturbing, both in the accuracy of the psychologist's predictions, the sexual violence it portrayed toward women, and its frequent use of four-letter words. All of us were aware that adolescents know and use such language. Still, it was jolting to have the graffiti read aloud to us and to realize that the authors were our own students. The climax was yet to come, however. After a long and embarrassing silence, one older male faculty member exclaimed: "I don't know what you are talking about with all this sex and violence stuff. All I know is, if I heard a kid on the athletic fields using such language, I'd knock his teeth down his throat." The point the psychologist was trying to make could hardly have been made any better if it was staged.

The separation of prep schools by sex occasionally led to sexist practices that were not only cruelly insensitive but silly. One female faculty interviewee told me of an all-male prep school that often raided her all-female school, located nearby, for "moonlighting" teachers for the male students. In two cases, the women teachers were used so much as moonlighters that they developed a feeling of being part of the male school community. The women were not allowed to march in the academic procession at commencement, however. When the older of the two retired, she petitioned that an exception be made for that year so she could do so. The petition was denied.

My study dealt only peripherally with gender difference perceptions as they related to school policies or campus atmosphere. In most cases, therefore, I had only a limited amount of data with which to work. Nonetheless, the results I was able to gather suggest that this issue may be central to the problems my study revealed. I shall have more to say on this issue shortly. The limited amount of feedback I did receive from both faculty and students on this issue suggests the following pattern:

First, all-female prep schools, especially if related to an all-male prep school, tend to reflect traditional concepts of the role of women in society. A student in one all-female school wrote that she and her friends noticed that:

> The arts and the humanities were stressed [whereas] the mathematics and sciences were very poor; the laboratory facilities were crummy . . . females were not supposed to excel in those areas.

In reflecting on this comment, I was reminded of a personal incident I experienced several years earlier. One of the benefits of teaching at Loomis Chaffee was that my children could attend tuition-free. Unfortunately, our oldest daughter was already two years into her high school education at a local all-female parochial school. Because she had formed close friendships with her classmates there, she did not want to leave; and we acquiesced to her wishes. The result, unfortunately, was that, though she would eventually go on to a university and receive both her bachelor's and master's degree (the latter with honors), she first had to attend a good two-year college for remedial work. In discussing this situation, a nun my husband met at a conference at Mt. Holyoke College commented, "I'll bet there is a boy's Catholic high school in the same town and that it has a better academic reputation." My husband agreed that this was correct. The nun went on to explain that Catholic schools were overseen by governing boards in which an all-male Church hierarchy decided the schools' education goals and criteria. Because girls were viewed as being of lesser value than boys, who were expected to be the breadwinners, when it came to who would receive the new microscopes, for example, they went to the boys' schools. The girls' schools got the old ones. The nun went on to point out that, in her experience, those Catholic girls' schools operating independently from their male counterparts were far better academically.

It may well be that this phenomenon is operative in the prep school described by the previous respondent. It would have been interesting to have the views of the women faculty at this school to include here, but I did not have the time to follow up on this issue. Theoretically, coeducation should solve the problem, because both female and male students not only have access to the same educational resources but also experience the same campus atmosphere. In practice this is not always the case. The merger of two schools to achieve coeducation had been carried out at most of the merged schools in my sample long before some of my student respondents arrived on campus. Yet many female students noted that they were soon made fully aware of the history of these mergers. As one put it:

> At [name of school] *no* traditions were preserved from
> the female school; nothing of it carried over into [name of
> school]. Thus there are very set male and female roles.

I did learn recently of one female school's tradition still re-
tained by the male school after a merger to achieve coeducation.
Kent School, in Kent, Connecticut, is a school with a "High
Church" Episcopalian background. Like Northfield Mount Hermon, the school was originally sex-segregated on campuses a few
miles apart. The now-coed Kent school still retains a " sacred kiss"
tradition involving "kiss lists" that contain the names of boys that
the junior girls must kiss in order to obtain their class rings. There
was great support by the males for retaining this tradition: "Haven't
the girls," went a student newspaper editorial, "lost enough traditions in the consolidated campus? . . . The girls have never been
forced to do something they didn't want to." From my own experience, English teacher Barbara Stout will probably find little
support for her view that "even though the seniors think that the
lists are done in good humor, they are done to purposely humili-
ate. The thing I detest is that it shows girls relating to boys in a
sexual way, pushing women's image back three centuries."

The previous student comment concerning set male and female
roles was reflected widely in several comments by both students
and faculty. Most serious, perhaps, was their detection of a double standard of discipline for males and females for certain kinds
of offenses. One student, obviously incensed by the injustice and
the thinking she perceived behind the decision, reported curtly:
"A girl caught in a boy's room got kicked out . . . it was because
she was in *his* room!"

The "boys will be boys but girls better not be that way" mentality also is evident. Many female faculty members were clearly
making efforts to deal with the problem, yet expressed concern
about the general campus atmosphere concerning their efforts. As
one put it:

> Next year the focus of the year will be on equality in edu-
> cation. We're opening the school year with a required

faculty workshop on sexism in education, using Carol Gilligan's book. It will help build awareness. There will be resentment, I know.

Another commented:

> My experience with both male faculty and students [suggests] that somehow books about males are universally interesting and significant, while books about females are interesting only to females. When at [name of school] I taught *Summer* by Edith Wharton, a wonderful novella about a girl growing up through discovering/appreciating her sexuality. The girls loved it; the boys thought it was "dumb," "mushy." Quite a few went so far as to rip the covers off their books because they were too embarrassed about carrying a book with flowers on the cover!

It would be unfair to blame all prep school male faculty members for instilling such machismo into the male students; but in my own experience, far too many do reinforce it. My husband recalls a conversation between two male faculty at lunch in the school dining hall when he was substitute teaching for me. One was decrying a protest march by women from the Women's Center at his alma mater that, when he was a student there, was all-male. The women were protesting his still all-male fraternity having carried out a panty raid. He referred to the protesters as "a bunch of dykes" and the male students who accompanied them as "pansies." The comment was made in the presence of students eating at the table and elicited no response from the other male faculty member.

The person who made this remark is a character type I have known at every prep school with which I have been associated. It is one with whom all prep school teachers are familiar: the jovial jock, a "one of the boys" type who usually is also "in" with the administration. That such faculty members feel free to use derogatory and bigoted language in front of colleagues and students shows how far short some of our schools have fallen from their stated ideals of respect for the dignity of all. I am not for a moment suggesting that teachers who see nothing wrong with using the terms *fairies*, *dykes*, or *pansies* would necessarily condone overt sexual exploitation or gay bashing. However, such persons cannot wash their hands of responsibility for helping to create an atmosphere in which such incidents may occur. Nor can any school administration escape culpability that considers whether a prospective faculty member can coach to be more important than whether that person is sexist or homophobic. Today, any prep school teacher who used the "N word" would be fired instantly. No less should be the case for those who use equally abusive terms describing gender or sexual orientation.

In schools that only recently became coeducational the difficulties of rooting out sexism were most evident. The suggestion that women faculty members were providing poor role models for female students appeared in rather diverse ways numerous times:

> Yes. . . there was. . . definitely sexism on the part of faculty members. There were a number of teachers who still held a lot of resentment for girls because the school had not been coed for very long.
>
> ***
>
> Everybody had to watch the male football team play — if they win, you get the next day off (!). But there is no female equivalent in athletics to football!
>
> ***
>
> In computer class there were no female models. One program used dealt with the buying and selling of wives (!). What was scary was that *the faculty was completely oblivious to its responsibility for establishing such a sexist atmosphere.* [emphasis added]

I think the term *oblivious* is the key word here. In a remarkably perceptive article written while she was still head of the Ethel Walker School, Margaret Huling Bonz cites a study of girls at the Laurel School in Cleveland, Ohio, noting that "adult women are co-conspirators with adolescent girls in promoting and maintaining the 'silence' and are skilled assistants in enabling girls not to know what they know." She goes on to quote former Laurel School Dean of Students Patricia Flanders Hall:

> It was first with a sense of shock and then a deep, knowing sadness that we listened to the voices of girls telling us that it was the adult women in their lives that provided the models for silencing themselves and behaving like "good little girls." We wept. . . we recognized what it was we had to do as teachers and mothers and therapists and women in relationship. Unless we, as grown women, were willing to give up all the "good little girl" things we continued to do and give up our expectation that the girls in our charge would be as good as we were, we could not successfully empower young women to act on their own knowledge and feelings. Unless we stopped hiding in expectations of goodness and control, our behavior would silence any words to girls about speaking in their own voice. (Gilligan and Brown 1992)

The feeling was expressed by some female faculty and students that there were few female faculty members who served as strong role models for the female students. More significant, hiring and promotion practices were viewed as selecting *against* such role models. As one student put it:

> Feminist consciousness and a female support system were just taken away because all these good people had left [name of school]. These people brought a lot of feelings to the surface. They were not so cold or far away as the rest of the faculty. There are few teachers you can really talk to at [name of school]. It has no support system for females; they are simply not used to dealing with females in the school.

If I were the head of a prep school and read such a comment by a student attending my school, I would want to call an emergency meeting of all parties concerned to ensure that it could never be written by any future students.

A series of questionnaire items for the students dealt with behavior and attitudes concerning sexual monogamy in their own relationships as well as for married persons. The results may have considerable significance for student perceptions of "proper" gender roles for both males and females. This was the only issue in which the attitudes of the prep school students in my sample were more "liberal" than their actual behavior. One question asked: "Approximately how many different people have you had sexual intercourse or activity with?" The question provided a scale from 0 to "more than 10." The results showed that the number of prep school students who had had sex with only one partner was significantly higher than for public school graduates. This was especially true with the prep school females; more than one-half reported being sexually monogamous as opposed to only one-quarter of the public school females. One possible reason for this, of course, is the strict faculty supervision of the prep school female, which acts to restrict access of both sexes to multiple partners. Another reason might be the intense social and academic pressure on female students in formerly all-male environments because, as I mentioned earlier, when prep schools become coeducational it is almost always the female school that moves to the male campus. As one female student respondent put it: "I'd say in general that sex took up precious energy needed to cope with the extreme academic pressure."

Many prep school female students accepted a double standard when it came to attitudes about having multiple sex partners. A statistically significant greater number of prep school females disapproved of both males and females having several sex partners than was the case with public school females. However, an equally significant number indicated that they would accept such behavior from the male they were "going with," though they admitted that, given the choice, they also would want many partners. Concerning extramarital sex, prep school students, especially the females, were significantly more liberal than their public school counterparts in rating this behavior acceptable for both husband and wife. (It is worth pointing out, I suppose, that prep school students often come from a socioeconomic group in which the frequency of extramarital sex is high.)

It is difficult to account for this inconsistency. On the one hand, they seem to accept what they view as the inevitability of promiscuity and even suggest they would abandon monogamy themselves. On the other hand, one gets the impression that if *they* could make the rules, rather than their male counterparts, they would opt for monogamy for both. Yet, if married, it seems they would accept promiscuity for both themselves and their spouses. One hypothesis to account for this might be that unmarried adolescent females in a highly competitive, male-oriented community desire the anchoring effect that a monogamous, "going steady" relationship might provide. Later, within a marriage relationship cemented by legal or religious affirmation, the need for sexual exclusiveness may be lessened. I confess that I have little confidence in this hypothesis or any others I have been able to devise. Far more research is needed before a clearer picture will emerge.

Questions about the use of drugs with sexual activity revealed a highly significant behavioral difference between prep school males and females and their public school counterparts. In terms of attitude, this difference prevailed among prep school males concerning taking sexual advantage of persons who were under the influence of drugs. *Almost one-quarter saw nothing wrong with this*, a figure nearly double that of the public school male sample. Most persons who would be taken sexual advantage of would be females. It is tempting, therefore, to suggest a relationship between the attitudes revealed here and those concerning politics and gender. The prep school males in my sample were significantly less supportive of equal rights for all, regardless of gender, than were public school males. One might, therefore, hypothesize that, if the prep school males who feel this way perceive females as unworthy of equal rights, then they may also see them as belonging to a group available for exploitation, be it sexual, economic, or otherwise. It also may be that the picture of insecurity and poor self-image that emerges from the prep school females' attitudes may account for their being significantly less supportive of equal rights for all, regardless of gender, than the public school females. That a poor self-image may characterize many prep school female students was suggested by many women faculty members in my sample:

Probably the biggest cause of sexism can be laid at the door of the girls themselves. They are the ones who look for, accept, and sometimes encourage male dominance. It is less so than before but still true. This is the way children are raised, to a lesser or greater degree, leaving them unconscious of the sexism around them. Of course they are supported in this by many adults, including many women members of our faculty.

***

In teaching an elective on women writers for 10-12 graders, I encountered a great deal of anti-feminist feelings, i.e., Oh God, Ms. [name], not another book in which men are insensitive clods who exploit women. When we showed the film "Killing Us Softly," I was shocked by how many girls thought that Joan Kilbourne had read too much into those ads and, even worse, thought that if sex and exploitation and violence against women occurs, well, too bad, that's the American way.

***

The boys are sexist and the girls play along, encouraging rather than correcting by failing to respond to this sexism. Of course, male faculty sexism provides a role model, as does the tendency to select the less feminist-oriented female faculty members for coaching.

The gender issue and prep school female self-image is a central, perhaps even key factor in dealing with the problems that are the focus of this book. As one female prep school teacher and reviewer of my manuscript wrote:

> I have to admit I find your results on preppie/public attitudes to equal rights both surprising and appalling. I would have expected more preppie females to support and expect equal rights.

I can think of no better way to end this chapter and underscore the importance of the issue with which this chapter deals than to cite an incident that occurred at a party I attended with my husband in Virginia. In the course of learning that a woman with whom he was conversing had attended one of the New England college preparatory schools in my study, my husband told her about my research. She made a beeline for me and related many experiences similar to those already shared with me by others. Her most telling point, however, was her comment (I had no tape recorder, so I can only paraphrase):

> The academic preparation [name of prep school] pro-
> vided put me at least a year ahead of my public school
> classmates in college. Its social preparation, however, left
> me two to three years behind and ripe for sexual exploita-
> tion. As a matter of fact, I *was* sexually exploited in my first
> year by an upperclassman dormitory advisor. I would never,
> ever, send my children to my prep school or, for that matter,
> any other.

CHAPTER 10

Sex, Education, and Values: Some Reflections

"There was only one faculty member I could speak to about personal matters. He was nonjudgmental, and open to new ideas. He would try to have students question more as to what they thought and encourage them to think for themselves rather than impose his values or those of the school on them. He made me feel that he respected me as much as I respected him."

— Student respondent

"Most people think of respect as obedience, submission to some higher authority that has more status, knowledge and skills. But respect is not about dutiful compliance to imposed rules from the top. . . . Real respect is a much more complex experience of empathy, trust and connection. It grows in relationship and has to be nourished every day."
— Sara Lawrence-Lightfoot, Harvard University (1999)

When I reread the title of my dissertation that helped spawn this book, "The Sexual Attitudes and Behavior of Private and Public School Students: A Comparative Study," it seemed so very dry. Emotionally immersed in the very world I was studying, I struggled to remain detached. Over and over my doctoral committee would drag me back on track, insisting that my data be firm, my statistics correct, my wording precise and objective. Often I failed; just as often, I was corrected. They were right, of course, and I am grateful.

Yet, somehow, somewhere, through all my data, I kept hearing the voices of the students. Many wrote between my objective questionnaire items or anywhere a small amount of space could be found, wanting to tell *their* story. Those that couldn't meet with me personally for interviews sent audiocassettes, so eager were they to be heard. Faculty, too, responded to a number and degree I would never have dreamed possible. When I read the one and only negative response to my faculty questionnaire — "We are not interested in this project" (sent back anonymously with no responses to any of the questionnaire items) — it seemed bizarre, almost incomprehensible: educators not interested in information that might make the institution they represent more effective?

Still, in some ways I understand. When lives are lived under one system of values and then those values are challenged, it is easier and far more comforting to simply withdraw. As one ages, reassurance becomes increasingly important. We need to hear that what we stood for is respected by those for whom we have been "teacher." To learn otherwise is unsettling. It is easier to go head-in-the-sand and hope for the best — at least until retirement.

I cannot do that. I am nowhere *near* "over the hill." I want this book, plus whatever energy I have left — and I have lots — to make a difference. I hope it will.

Yet, I also have fears. I fear that some will say, "Her sample was not large enough." One reviewer of this manuscript, a prep school English teacher, said just that. In fact, according to two of my statistical advisors, it was needlessly large. Considering the available pool, my sample was far larger than the one used to predict, with astonishing accuracy, the percentage of President Ronald Reagan's victory over Walter Mondale in 1984.

I fear some might just say, "The students *I'm* around would never say or do such things!" (Of course they wouldn't — not while *you're* around!) That, of course, is both the beauty and ugliness of research. The beauty comes from the knowledge that, properly done, one finds out what is really going on. The ugliness results from the fact that the truth often hurts.

Most of all, I fear that what these students are telling us will cause the knee-jerk reaction to which all of us who are or have been in prep school life too easily succumb. The headmaster who learns from this book that his school's athletic fields, woods, or chapel are the most common areas for student sexual activity and immediately proceeds to assign faculty patrols to those areas has missed the point entirely. So a few more violators will be caught and humiliated. What, pray tell, will *that* solve? As a lesson to others? Certainly. But *what* lesson?

In science there is a saying: Nature never tells a lie, but sometimes she answers a question you didn't know you were asking. So it is with teaching values: We think we are imparting one set, but our students may be perceiving quite another. Beyond that, we live in an Alvin Toffler age of "future shock." Until very recently in human history, the "eternal truths" at one's birth were the same at death. Now we see them changing all around us and feel insecure. Historians Vern and Bonnie Bullough have suggested why this may be so:

> Though Copernicus, Darwin, and Freud started trends of thought which undermined previous assumptions about the nature of man and his place in the world, they basically left intact the assumptions about moral conduct, much of which was based upon an aversion to sexuality. The sexual revolution, however, challenges this basic foundation of Western thought. This is because the ongoing research into sex has undermined much of the basis for the belief that sex is evil, and in the process has challenged assumptions about premarital, marital, and extramarital sex, as well as attitudes about non-procreative sex which societies in the past have stigmatized as being deviant. The research has also indicated that mankind, or at least the Western version of it, has sought to keep itself uncomfortable and full of anxiety by emphasizing the sinful nature or the inherent sickness of those who engage in an active sex life. (1975, pp. 224–25)

That the prep school world is caught in the midst of this revolution is perhaps best illustrated by the following examples, the first and third of which were provided by my student respondents. The first example is:

> One dorm counselor talked to us about "alternative" forms
> of sexual gratification that do not risk pregnancy. She was on
> our side and implicitly condoned placating the school by
> obeying the letter of the law and violating its spirit.

We are not informed what these alternative forms are. There
are several possibilities, of course; the list is limited only by the
human imagination. We know from research data that masturbation and other forms of sexual gratification short of intercourse
are widespread in the United States and elsewhere. Yet, as the
Bulloughs point out, until very recently (and, in some cases, even
today) all have been condemned as "unnatural" or "perverted" by
traditional Judeo-Christian teachings precisely *because* they present no possibility of pregnancy.

This being the case, is what this counselor is doing wrong?
Most certainly this student did not think so. If wrong, does it lie
in the counselor conveying to the students contempt for a school
rule by violating its spirit? Should she instead fight from within
to change the rule and, in the meantime, tell the students to obey
it? What is the proper value to adopt here?

The second example is of a slightly different sort. A problem
for many prep schools has been graduation-week parties thrown
by parents for their daughter or son and their friends. Because
many if not most prep school students come from families in which
the parents drink alcoholic beverages, cocktails or wine and beer
may be served. The results are predictable. Shielded from alcohol
at school (though, of course, they get and use it anyway) the students are not skilled social drinkers and become intoxicated. I do
not know how many lives have been lost in automobile accidents
following such events; I do know that there were several during
the years I taught. Presumably learning from the experience of
hearing of students killed or left handicapped for life, some parents giving such parties have adopted the practice of collecting
the car keys at the door. I think most would agree this is a responsible thing to do.

But now consider the following comment from another respondent, which will serve as example three: A student conveyed the

story of "a student's mother who placed condoms in a dish when parties were given for students in her home."

How about *that* one? Surely no reader of this book can be unaware that many opposing such an action would say that the mother was being irresponsible. She is, it is often maintained, not only condoning premarital sex but actually encouraging immoral behavior. (How often has Planned Parenthood heard that time-worn argument?) Others would say that, by recognizing that sexual desire is a natural and healthy aspect of young adulthood and that an unwanted pregnancy could ruin promising young lives, this mother was showing a high level of parental responsibility, both for her daughter or son and their friends. As the Kent school student on the pro side of her school supplying condoms debate suggested in a previous chapter, in the age of AIDS when serious illness or death may result, *not* to provide access to protection may well be immoral. This case and the previous one amply support the Bulloughs' claim: The responses we give to such cases are no longer unanimous because the value assumptions that once served as the underpinnings of this unanimity are now suspect.

There is another aspect of the sexual revolution that is equally significant and powerful. Cultural and religious myths, as well as the moral teachings that stem from them, almost always sustain rather than challenge the economic and political structures in which they thrive. As feminist Adrienne Rich points out, compulsory heterosexuality (and, she might have added, monogamy) has served as one of the main means by which the right of physical, economic, and emotional ownership of women by men is guaranteed. My impression is that most feminists would argue that social equality of the sexes will never be complete as long as men continue to dominate the economic, political, and religious arenas. Until this power imbalance is corrected, sex may always be used as a means of exercising control. As educators, we must be fully cognizant of this if we are to tap into the maximum potential of our female students. As Ethel Walker School's Margaret Huling Bonz put it:

> Cultural norms propagated and maintained by a patriarchal
> society continue to deprive the world of precious and valuable
> resources. Given the enormity of problems facing the global
> community, we can ill afford this wasting of human potential
> . . . we must identify ways to encourage " resistance" among
> our young women so that they may grow into confident adults
> with strong, persistent voices. (1993, p. 5)

One student told me of her school's headmaster addressing the student body and making the statement: "If you are sexually active, you do not belong at this school." I thought at the time that the statement was a recent one. Later, however, a woman law student who had graduated from the school seven years earlier repeated the same statement to me word for word. Clearly, the statement had enough impact and staying power to be passed on to later students as they entered the school. The reaction of the older student to the statement was one of indignation and contempt. She wrote:

> They should have put on the [name of school] applications
> a statement, like the nineteenth century job applications that
> read "no Irish need apply," that no non–virgins need apply!

The reaction of the younger student, still attending the school, was merely one of amusement.

Proceeding from the assumption that the headmaster's words were as reported, I have thought long and hard about them. To be fair, I have tried to imagine in what possible context they might have been expressed so as to make any sense at all. I can think of none. I asked myself what he could possibly mean by " sexually active"? *All* human beings are sexually active, before birth — male fetuses have erections and female fetuses' vaginas lubricate — until death. Does he mean masturbate? If so, he'd have virtually no students or faculty. Does he mean those who are no longer virgins? According to my data, by commencement he would lose three-fourths of the males in the graduating class and almost two-thirds of the females. What sort of effect does a statement like that make on an adolescent for whom the headmaster is supposed to be a role model? The woman law student could still recall her own reaction and that of her classmates: "We were *appalled!*" Whatever that headmaster meant by his comment, it is what the statement conveyed to the students in his audience that is significant.

In precisely the same manner, it is the values that prep schools convey by their actions and examples that count, not what they state publicly about their value systems. When a school states that it affirms the essential goodness of a healthy sexuality and then proceeds to create an environment in which such a sexuality is impossible, the students are not fooled one bit. As humiliating as it was to read in my student respondents' comments, they see such attitudes as *our* problem, not theirs. One student, whose expressed love for his prep school was obviously deep and gen-uine, still found it necessary to write:

> We were like rats in a cage, deprived of a normal life of varied sensory stimuli by the cruel design of the cage itself, which forced its occupants to walk a never-ending treadmill of study and athletics. As a result, whenever the treadmill allowed us rare respite, we attacked whatever of the cage's bars we could find to gnaw. We did so clumsily; aimlessly, for our masters had provided us no training in how to do it otherwise. They taught us to be students; they taught us to be athletes; they did not teach us how to be sensitive, sexu-al, caring human beings. Those of us who became so did so in spite of the school, not because of it. I do not now blame the faculty for this, for I have come to understand that, with notable exceptions, they, themselves, had never learned how, and the prospect of their doing so, or seeing their students do so, must have seemed terrible to them.

One faculty comment was of particular interest to me:

> Filling it [the questionnaire] out reminded me that at my boarding school we were taught about chastity, self-restraint, and "purity" — meaning the self-exercised control of the sexual impulse. Your questionnaire gives no space to the presence of these and similar teachings. Yet self-restraint is both desired and desirable, and perhaps the oldest established

method of regulating sexuality and helping people to control self-indulgence. It is not to be confused with repression.

In truth, this was the sort of comment I expected to see more often. (It was the only one, though others holding such views may well not have responded.) To me, this person is wrong. Such teaching *is* repressive. Most certainly, as a pre-Vatican II-trained Roman Catholic, I am familiar with the philosophy expressed by this writer. Such views are associated historically with the period of reactionary Christian asceticism of the second, third, and fourth centuries, especially the views of St. Augustine of Hippo (353-430 C.E.) and their later distillation in the 13th century by St. Thomas Aquinas. Of course, as Roman Catholic adolescents we knew nothing of this. We were told only that God wanted us to be like the Virgin Mary, "pure, immaculate, undefiled." Even thoughts about that "forbidden pleasure" were labeled "impure." My mother made me a dress for my one parochial high school's senior-year tea dance dates with a boy I was most eager to impress. Unfortunately, the dress was one of those off-the-shoulder designs popular in the 1940s. A nun saw me going downstairs to meet my date. Horrified, she pinned the *New York Times* over my shoulders and made me dance attired in that manner for the entire evening!

As I look back on that incident, I am less angry at that nun than I am at a system of thought that would teach that such humiliation of an adolescent was a proper thing to do and, far worse, make me so accepting of it. At the all-woman Catholic college I attended, the strong impression was conveyed that, unless we were constantly on guard, we would commit a small, or "venial," sin that would inevitably lead us into a serious, or "mortal," sin. "A girl who will smoke is a girl who will drink, and a girl who will drink is a girl who will do anything" is the way a nun who caught me smoking a cigarette put it. And, mind you, this was in college. Unfortunately, precisely the same sort of thinking comes across in the way prep schools are handling their students' sexuality.

To return to the comment previously quoted for a moment, of course "self-restraint" is a desirable attribute in human activity, including eating, drinking, *and* sexual expression. My point, however, is that during my schooling (and, I suspect, that of the respondent) there was a hidden agenda — the control of female sexuality — with all the social and economic benefits to males that such control provides. To just such hidden agendas is former Miss Porter's School head Rachel Belash referring in her comment that was quoted in Chapter 4. These hidden agendas simply *must* be brought out into the open for uninhibited discussion if we are truly to educate, rather than merely to indoctrinate.

By now I would hope that my prep school readers are feeling a tinge of annoyance, feeling that I have been long on criticism of the prep schools' handling of student sexuality and related matters but short on concrete recommendations concerning change. I can hear it now: "What would you have us do, give them freedom to be alone together whenever they could?"

As shocking as it may appear, my answer to that question is: Yes. There are some very big "ifs" to be taken care of first, however.

To begin, let us put things in perspective. Even if these "ifs" are not taken care of and my "freedom plan" were adopted, from the perspective of the schools' own stated values, things are probably not going to get much worse. After all, 75% of prep school males and 60% of prep school females is a fair amount of lost virginity. While the idea of allowing private time may seem radical, one of my faculty respondents suggests that his school already has taken steps in that direction. In response to my question dealing with faculty reactions on encountering students involved in sexual activity, this person wrote:

> In formal or informal ways [name of school] faculty learn to be very protective of student privacy, [and] therefore the likelihood of encountering a student in the performance of any sexual act is very slim. As a dorm resident or head (seven years) and as a dean I have no recollection of any students (maybe one instance) being encountered in the act . . . students have a lot of time between a knock on the door and an acknowledgment to enter.

Such a policy shows a genuine respect for the student as an individual.

There also are some factors that must be considered "givens." Central to the issue here is that human beings are sexual beings, and attempts to express that part of their personhood are natural, normal, and healthy. Since adolescence marks a blooming of this expression in more adult ways, this applies especially to this age group. As I noted earlier, research in the developmental and behavioral sciences has shown that the old "nature versus nurture" dichotomy between innate and learned behaviors is, quite simply, meaningless. We now recognize that, like the developing limb of an embryo, all behaviors, including sexual, are such a fine mosaic of genetic and environmental factors that it is virtually impossible to separate one from the other. One can, of course, experimentally expose a developing embryo's limb bud to certain physical or chemical agents and, depending on the stage of development, produce predictable deformities. With a human embryo and fetus, we wish the development to be as healthy and normal as possible, and therefore we attempt to provide a prenatal environment that will maximize the chances of normality. When the newborn infant appears, we watch the thrashing movements of its arms and legs. Somewhat later we note with pride its clumsy attempts to grasp objects. No one would think of restraining these movements, waiting until the child was, say, six years old and could "responsibly" hold objects. Instead, we encourage the movements, accepting their clumsiness as natural. We encourage their refinement until, with unbridled joy, we see the parental finger held, the rattle shaken.

We do not do so with sexuality. We seem stuck in the old instinctive mode of action. Traditional morality of the sort mentioned by the writer who stressed "purity" and resistance to "self-indulgence" taught young people to avoid all forms of physical contact that might lead to "impure thoughts" or "desires of the flesh." Yet, once married, the couple was expected to know exactly what to do: "Nature" will tell them! What happens is as predictable as it would be if one restrained an infant's arms until adulthood. Like the honeymooning couple, its actions would be awkward, revealing clear signs of being handicapped. Eventually, like the couple, it might succeed and, if fortunate, learn what should have been learned years before.

Those who read into the preceding the suggestion that I am recommending total freedom of sexual expression for prep school or any other adolescents are missing the point entirely. When my own infants were first learning to grasp objects, I did not give them sharp knives with which to play. Such objects, with proper practice, are highly useful; without that practice, potentially dangerous. I did, however, let them try grasping rattles. In the same vein, like sharp objects, sexual intercourse carries with it the capacity for hurt, most notably unwanted pregnancy, with the unpleasant alternatives of abortion or premature parenthood. Furthermore, it is not an evenly shared hurt; all too often, the male partner has the option of walking away from the situation; the female cannot. For these and other reasons, I am unequivocally opposed to sexual intercourse for adolescents. I certainly recognize there are exceptional adolescents with the emotional maturity to handle such involvement. But I am convinced that this number is small. I therefore prefer to make my statement a blanket one rather than equivocate on such an important matter.

On the other hand, to return to my infant analogy, what I *am* suggesting is that we leave our students free to thrash their arms and legs around in a safe (that is, nonexploitative), nurturing, and information-rich environment. More prep school faculty members are needed like the one described by the student quoted at the start of this chapter. However, I would not allow this degree of freedom at any school until the following criteria were met:

1. Every female student should be required to take courses or seminars in feminist and postfeminist thought. Such instruction would include both theory and practice, the psychology of womanhood in a patriarchal society, and the practice of assertiveness within that context. The same sort of exposure would be beneficial to the male students (and faculty) as well. At this point, however, attention should be focused on the group that is most vulnerable to sexual exploitation and its aftermath, the female

students. With increasing sophistication throughout the four years, I would make certain that each student continued her exposure through literature, seminars, and classes.

Why? I noted in the last chapter that many of my women faculty respondents placed much of the blame for the large amount of exploitative sexual activity at their schools on the shoulders of the prep school females. They also cited poor role models provided them by far too many women faculty members. (Recall that many of my faculty respondents suggested that prep schools select against assertiveness in women faculty in promotion to administrative positions.) My own impressions and research results are consonant with this viewpoint. I suggest that a policy of allowing maximum freedom within the context of a school filled with female students exposed to such information would be far more successful in controlling sexual activity than the vast amount of faculty energy expended under policies that were in vogue when I was teaching and, in many cases, still are the norm. It might also ensure that the sexual activity that did occur would be of a sort far healthier than my data indicate. I recognize that the danger inherent in my stress on limiting such classes to female students may be to perpetuate the myth that they alone are responsible for protecting themselves. One might almost as easily argue that it is the male students who need such a course of study.

2. An up-to-date class in human sexuality should be required of all students. Further — and this is most important — it should be offered by the science department, though such placement would not preclude others from contributing to it. This type of class has been offered by the Middlesex School in Concord, New Hampshire, for some years. A 1987 catalogue description of this course reads:

> Science 2. *Human Sexuality*. . . .Topics include human reproduction and development, adolescent behavior patterns, and issues brought up in the normal course of class discussion. The emphasis is on understanding problems students encounter as they grow physically and emotionally into adults.

Most departments probably do not have anyone qualified to teach such a course. Thus a qualified individual should be hired or an opportunity should be provided to a member of the science department to begin the necessary study to become qualified.

Since first writing this recommendation in the late 1980s, I was pleased to see that Dr. Margaret Huling Bonz included almost precisely the same recommendation in her 1993 article concerning the education of young women. She wrote:

> Equally important is comprehensive, upbeat education about sexuality. Information about contraception, sexually transmitted disease, sexual development, sexual decision making, sexual orientation, and women's physiology and health must be systematically and sympathetically conveyed. Essential as it is to acquaint young women fully with the potential for abuse and victimization, they need assurances that non-coercive, non-exploitative sexual relationships are normal and healthy. Robinson emphasizes the importance of "preparing" rather than "protecting" our girls and of establishing school based health centers and comprehensive health education programs in our schools. According to Robinson, adult women have a special responsibility to talk, i.e., not remain silent, to teach about these matters, and to create an environment that enables girls to resist conventional forms of femininity. (1993, pp. 8–9)

3. The entire school community should bring its "sexual agenda" out in the open. If homophobia exists, as it almost surely does, deal with it openly and honestly. All too often, directives concerning new school policies come from the school head or the board of trustees. For example, in the Spring 1994 *Andover Bulletin*, the Phillips Andover trustees recommended that the administration name an advisor for gay and lesbian students and that it "establish a benefits policy for committed gay and lesbian partners, to define this commitment and to study a change in policy to allow these partners *in non-dormitory housing*" (p. 21, emphasis added). As enlightened as this policy may appear on the surface, serious problems lie ahead if the entire community was

not involved in the discussions that led to it. Homophobia, especially if religiously based, is not confronted in a constructive manner by administrative directives. Instead, it merely goes underground, often to surface in more virulent and destructive ways.

As I stated, in my faculty survey each person was asked the question: "In general, what do you think a faculty member's response would be upon discovering two students engaged in heterosexual intercourse?" They were then asked, " What would be your own response?" to the same situation. Similar questions were asked concerning masturbation and homosexual activity. By far the most interesting result was that, *without a single exception*, each of the respondents viewed his or her own reaction as being far more tolerant and understanding than they felt would be the case with his or her faculty colleagues.*

The importance of this finding simply cannot be overemphasized. It suggests that many of the serious problems perceived by both students and faculty at their schools might be resolved if the schools simply worked to create an atmosphere that allowed faculty members to speak openly on school policies. Given the information provided by my student and faculty respondents, such action is long overdue. A good school should foster positive interpersonal communication. Yet, from what I read in my respondents' comments, these very good schools are not doing so. If, in fact, the typical prep school is, as one faculty interviewee described her school, "a stiff, conservative, bug-up-the-behind type of community," it is time for a change.

A good start might be to diminish the power of the head and proportionally increase that of the academic faculty. Hiring practices should select for academic and teaching excellence in conjunction with an assertive professionalism. By professionalism, I mean a faculty unafraid to speak out publicly on such issues as academics versus athletics, gender discrimination, school policies

---

*It is important to stress again that my follow-up survey included only faculty members, not administrators.

concerning the use of drugs, student social and sexual intimacy, and so on — with individuals strong enough to refuse to subvert their own value systems and behavior to the sort of collective value systems proclaimed by their schools. By so doing, we provide our students with a pluralistic view of society that engenders tolerance and respect for individual differences. Were faculty allowed to express openly the ideas those in my sample shared with me privately, many of the problems I have pinpointed in these pages might be resolved.

There is nothing intrinsically wrong with prep school students because they may be more sexually active and sophisticated than their public school counterparts. Rather, it is the reasons they give for so being that are disturbing. For both males and females there is the excitement of challenging often ridiculous school rules and succumbing to peer pressure to do so; for males, an expression of the athletic "coolness" they perceive many of the faculty as favoring. Worse, for the females, such behavior is viewed as a means of gaining attention from the group they perceive as holding all the power, the males. Joan Jacob Brumberg, in *The Body Project: An Intimate History of American Girls,* offers a useful perspective. Brumberg notes, "Girls who do not feel good about themselves need the affirmation of others, and that, unfortunately, almost always empowers male desire." Brumberg interprets this (correctly, I believe) to mean that "girls . . . do not make good decisions about the kind of sexual activity that is in their best interest."

I implied earlier that the results of my study comparing the sexual behavior and attitudes of prep school and public school students might well be a shock to most prep school faculty and administrators. There are value judgments involved in such an implication, of course. However, recall that at the outset my study stressed the prep school emphasis on the inculcation of values in their students. I know of no college preparatory school that would view a high degree of sexual activity in combination with drug use as consistent with the values it was trying to inculcate. If only 1% of prep school males saw nothing wrong with taking sexual advantage of a person under the influence of drugs, it would be an unacceptably high figure; that the actual percentage is almost 25% surely indicates that *something* is seriously wrong. As for the prep school females, almost one-third report having been sexually exploited in this manner. If, indeed, our prep schools are imparting values, we must ask ourselves just what sort of values they are.

As I noted in Chapter 9, one of the findings of my study was that both prep school male and female students were less supportive of equal rights for all regardless of sex than were their public school counterparts. This last result was particularly distressing to me. I had always assumed that most aspire to a nonsexist world of gender equality and that one important pathway toward achieving this goal lies through our education institutions. From the picture painted by these data, prep schools might be perceived as institutions more to be blamed than nurtured. I believe that such a conclusion would be in error.

I taught and carried out my research during a transitional time in the history of college prep schools, a time during which they were showing signs of moving from the elitist status they once enjoyed toward applying the considerable skills and resources they have always possessed to pressing social issues. The move to coeducation at previously all-male schools has certainly been one major factor in bringing about change. Had my study been done thirty years earlier, one might predict that the results would have revealed prep school views of women, sexuality, and so forth, that reflected an entirely male-oriented view of the world, whether the research was done at Deerfield Academy for Boys or Miss Porter's School for Girls. As many male faculty recognized (and thus often resisted), the entry of female students and faculty into their domains marked the end of the era of total control by males. There is reason to hope a similar study, done two decades hence, will reveal a far more encouraging picture. Indeed, just the integration of women into these schools is causing them, as Carol Gilligan (1982) might put it, to speak "in a different voice."

If the move toward coeducation has lessened the degree of sexism at college preparatory schools, no less may it serve to encourage the growth of a healthier view of sexuality. In the areas of sexism and homophobia, it would be interesting to design a research study that would compare such attitudes at coeducational and all-male or all-female college preparatory schools, with the study including faculty as well as students.

Let me now move beyond the area of sexual attitudes and behavior, to which my study was limited, and move into the larger context of possibilities for education philosophy and reform.

Prep schools simply must learn to stop being so caught up in their own rhetoric about education and values formation that they react to implied criticism in a highly defensive, almost paranoid manner. The CBS documentary show, *60 Minutes,* on a Choate-Rosemary Hall/Emma Willard School drug bust incident that I mentioned earlier, provides a case in point. "While it is a fact that drugs in schools are an everyday problem, Choate does not present itself as an everyday school," said commentator Ed Bradley. Indeed, it doesn't. Nor do the other schools in my study. As I have repeatedly pointed out, prep schools stress their uniqueness in inculcating values. Trapped in their own rhetoric, when a school is caught in what it perceives as an embarrassing failure to inculcate these values, the first moves are designed to keep this failure out of the public eye. One prep school teacher expressed to me his observation (and that of many of his colleagues) of a tendency among prep schools, on learning that one of their female students was pregnant, to counsel her that she would undoubtedly feel "more comfortable" if she transferred to another school. He stated flatly his opinion that it was not the student's welfare being protected, but rather the school "covering its own ass."

Similarly, in the case of the Choate-Rosemary Hall/Emma Willard drug bust, it is difficult to avoid the feeling that both schools responded to the crisis in a manner designed to protect their own self-image rather than the well-being of their students. The tragic suicide of one of the expelled students is perhaps the most dramatic example, but there are others. (At one school where I taught, a student was coolly receiving drugs through the mail to sell on campus. By some rather deft management, the school managed to keep it out of the newspapers.) The remarks of one *60 Minutes* Choate-Rosemary Hall student interviewee suggest that his school would have garnered a great deal more respect if it had brought the matter "out in the open and not worry about their reputation of being a perfect school where they have no problems, because that's really not being realistic."

Unfortunately, "bringing it out in the open" is precisely what prep schools have been most reluctant to do; historically, they have been far better at patting themselves on the back than engaging in serious self-examination and criticism.

Encouragingly, a model for a self-criticizing prep school was proposed by Northfield Mount Hermon headmaster Richard Unsworth in his school's 1985-86 annual report. He acknowledged that his school has "entwined certain traditional values" in its curriculum, but went on to state:

> A tradition cannot simply be inherited. If it is to remain a continuing force in changing times, *it must be risked and re-created through time.* In our culture, this must begin in the schools. (p. 3, emphasis added)

Yet self-criticism is difficult for schools that engage in intense competition with other schools for applicants. This factor tends to ensure that self-aggrandizing behavior is reinforced. Headmaster John Rae is quite open and explicit concerning this:

> Beware! Headmasters are among the best con men in the business. If we were not running schools we would be selling London Bridge to American tourists. We are not trying to deceive you, just to pull the wool over your eyes. It is our job to present our schools in the best possible light and most of us are pretty good at it. Parents are predisposed to believe what a headmaster says; it is hard to associate the dark suits, the boyish faces and the streaks of silver hair with the morals of Madison Avenue. The popular misconception that headmasters are out of touch with the harsh realities of the market place gives us an edge.

The first thing to understand about the schools is that they are in competition with one another. With independent schools that can be cut-throat. The motto of the independent sector should be La Rochefoucauld's famous aphorism "In the misfortune of our best friends, we find something that is not displeasing to us." The scandals that rock your competitors are a matter for public sympathy and private satisfaction. (1987, p. 217)

Former Phillips Exeter principal Kendra Stearns O'Donnell also recognizes this problem. From what I have read, O'Donnell seems to have brought to her school a remarkable perceptiveness concerning the tendency of prep schools to be so captivated by their own promotional rhetoric that they accept it as dogma. At a March 1988 225th Founding Anniversary Conference at Governor Dummer Academy dealing with the future of college preparatory school education, she remarked:

> I would hope that our reaction to Mr. Snelling's nice facts would not draw us outward but would encourage us to look inward. The craze about marketing is all very well — the process of deciding what we want to say about ourselves to an audience — as long as we check the reality of what we are saying. We are promoting ourselves as environments where kids learn not only in the classroom but they learn within a community. They learn values, they learn standards, they learn and grow morally as well as intellectually. I think we are challenged to make sure that's true.

I could not agree more. However, in these schools' desire to exemplify their values, we must make certain that our schools adopt policies that truly respect individual differences. Like many school administrators, Joanne Hoffman, former associate head of Concord Academy, speaks of "values central to this complex school." She then goes on to describe Concord as a place where:

> learning for its own sake and differences in perspective are welcomed, tested, and celebrated. . . . During the high school years, adolescents typically struggle to find their voice, to forge their identity intellectually, emotionally, and

physically. At this age, students need to test many voices, to
look at many templates, to experiment with a variety of
"selves" enroute to finding a truer, more dependable self.
This process needs to happen in a place that supports the
search for that authenticity rather than [one that] offers a
"one size fits all" approach. (1994, pp. 2-4)

My prep school teaching career, spanning 34 years, has left me
with only one feeling: I love prep schools. I love even more what
they could so easily become — pioneers in creating a genuinely
healthy environment for adolescent mental and physical development. From what I read in many prep school magazines, powerful steps are being taken in just this direction. For example:

With adequate support, we can take on the challenges. We
can take on learning styles and technology, sexuality issues
and substance abuse, power and harassment, college
demands and diversity. (Wilcox 1995, p. 6)

I can think of no better way to close this book than to quote
from a former college preparatory school head, now deceased,
who I knew only through her writings. In a personal note to me
after reviewing my manuscript and making many helpful suggestions, she wrote:

Whatever the flaws in most private schools, they are
worlds better than most and should be encouraged and
helped and loved in any way we all can. The ignorance all
around me breaks the heart.

A Final Thought

My husband, the author of a book on the American Civil War,
brought to my attention a quote from William H. Herndon,
Abraham Lincoln's long-time friend and law partner in the years
before he became president. The year after Lincoln's assassina-
tion, Herndon announced his intention to write a biography of his
friend. Yet, knowing personal information about the president,
including sexual exploits, that conflicted with a rapidly growing
and sanctifying myth, Herndon found himself 20 years later hav-

ing written hardly a word. As he explained, "To tell the truth — the exact truth as you see it — is a hard road to travel in this world when that truth runs square up against what our ideas of what we think *ought* to be."

In a somewhat similar vein, writing in the 10 September 1995 Sunday *New York Times Book Review* concerning Albert J. Raboteau's book, *A Fire in the Bones: Reflections on African-American Religious History*, Rembert G. Weakland notes that the author "does what is dangerous for a historian: he combines history with a personal journey."

Both Herndon and Weakland are right concerning the dangers. No less is the case for what I have done here, combining objective research results with personal and admittedly highly subjective reflections on matters I perceive as being related to those results. In an epilogue to my dissertation, which was the basis of this book, I wrote:

> From the standpoint of the ideal of an unbiased observer, it is wrong, I suppose, for a person who has spent so much of her professional and personal life in the prep school world to undertake a study of this sort. Total objectivity is a goal often strived for and, according to historians and philosophers of science, rarely, if ever, achieved in research. Nonetheless, I have tried to do my best in this regard and take comfort in the fact that, since these data did not reveal what I might have preferred, perhaps the intellectual integrity of my research will be accepted. I would be rewarded beyond measure should it suggest other areas of study to those who might care to follow.

No less applies to this book. I have tried to present, as faithfully as possible, what I felt my student and faculty respondents were telling me.

Appendices

Schools in the Study

Sixteen prep schools were included in the study that forms the basis for this book. Most are all-male schools; the exceptions are noted. All but one school are located in New England. Alphabetically, the schools are:

Choate-Rosemary Hall, a coeducational school composed of the former Choate, all-male, and Rosemary Hall, all-female, schools; located in Wallingford, Connecticut.

Concord Academy, located in Concord, Massachusetts.

Deerfield Academy, all-male at the time of the study but now coed, located in Deerfield, Massachusetts.

Emma Willard, all-female and the only school outside New England to be included in the study; located in Troy, New York.

Groton Academy, located in Groton, Massachusetts.

Gunnery School, located in Washington, Connecticut.

Hotchkiss School, located in Lakeville, Connecticut.

Kent, located in Kent, Connecticut.

Loomis Chaffee School, a coeducational school composed of the former Loomis, all-male, and Chaffee, all-female, schools; located in Windsor, Connecticut.

Miss Porter's, all-female, located in Farmington, Connecticut.

Northfield Mount Hermon, a coeducational school composed of the former Mount Hermon, all-male, and Northfield, all-female, schools; located in Northfield, Massachusetts.

Phillips Academy, Andover (Andover, Massachusetts), often referred to as Phillips Andover or just Andover.

Phillips Academy, Exeter (Exeter, New Hampshire), often referred to as Phillips Exeter or just Exeter.

St. Paul's, located in Concord, New Hampshire.

Taft, located in Watertown, Connecticut.

Williston, located in Northampton, Massachusetts.

Research Methods and Findings

In his *New Republic* review of Edward O. Wilson's book, *Consilience: The Unity of Knowledge*, Tzvetan Todorov notes:

> The social sciences . . . are not exactly flourishing these days, at least in the good sense. Their practitioners are usually content to dress up their common sense in technical — that is, incomprehensible — terms, by attaching it to long and expansive statistical inquiries. In the best cases, they are communicating an intuited truth about their subject, but [it is] a highly unscientific truth, a truth that cannot be turned into a formula. (27 April 1998, p. 29)

Especially concerning my work described in this book, I heartily agree. It was partly in an attempt to avoid this perception that I made a deliberate choice to use "many," or "the majority," and so forth, in reporting my results. So doing also enabled me to avoid having to use such cumbersome language as "83.1% of prep school students responded affirmatively in contrast to 54.6% of their public school counterparts, the difference being significant to the 0.005 level." While, as a person trained in science, I might personally prefer such precision, I felt that its use throughout the book would result in its not being read by the audience I was most eager to reach, as well as imply in my results an absolute certainty unattainable in the social sciences or, for that matter, in most other sciences. In this appendix I present my data and those relevant researches of others in a manner that may be helpful to others who might want to repeat my work or some modification thereof.

Historical Perspective

In order to put my study of the sexual attitudes and behavior of college-bound prep school and public school graduates in proper perspective, it is necessary to place research on human sexuality in general into some sort of historical framework. While there were many pioneers in the field in the late 19th and early 20th centuries (for example, Iwan Bloch, Havelock Ellis, and Sigmund Freud) most of their writings, as insightful as they may have been, were based on subjective analyses of clinical cases and lacked a solid empirical base. One of the most complete empirically based scientific studies of human sexuality was carried out in Germany in the early years of the 20th century by Magnus Hirschfeld. Unfortunately, Hirschfeld's Institute in Berlin was raided in 1933 by the Nazis, who destroyed all of his files and burned his books. Hirschfeld, a Jew, was fortunately out of the country at the time. He died in exile in France two years later.

Research on human sexuality in the United States is usually dated from the publication of the so-called Kinsey Reports, in actuality two massive volumes, *Sexual Behavior of the Human Male* (1948), by Alfred C. Kinsey, Wardell B. Pomeroy, and Clyde Martin, and *Sexual Behavior of the Human Female* (1953), in which the Kinsey group was joined by Paul H. Gebhard. The research team was based at Indiana University. In Kinsey's studies the ages of the subjects sampled ranged from pre-adolescent to elderly. The research dealt almost exclusively with sexual behaviors, rather than attitudes. It is important to note that the Kinsey team's subjects did not constitute a probability sample, containing, for example, an over-representation of college students, Protestants, and residents of Indiana and the Northeastern United States. No blacks were included. Nor did these studies deal with adolescents *per se* but tended to focus on data pertinent to those years of human development only insofar as they contributed to an overall picture of adult human sexual behavior in general. Later research focused largely on subset groups of the larger population involved in the Kinsey studies, such as preadolescents or senior citizens.*

Among such studies are those dealing with adolescents. By far the most noteworthy for my purposes were those of Robert C. Sorensen (*Adolescent Sexuality in Contemporary America*, 1973) and Aaron Hass (*Teenage Sexuality: A Survey of Teenage Sexual Behavior,* 1979). Both Sorensen and Hass dealt specifically with the sexual behavior *and attitudes* of adolescents, and their results were reported within the decade preceding my own research. Thus they provided me with far more directly comparable results than did the strictly behavioral, mostly volunteer interview research of Kinsey and his colleagues. I was able to have only informal conversations with Hass, but the presence of both Pomeroy and Sorensen (most especially the latter) on my doctoral dissertation committee was of immeasurable help. (Pomeroy had by this time left Indiana University and moved to the Institute for the Advanced Study of Human Sexuality in San Francisco, where I was able to work with him.) Two other persons, Lewis Durham and the late Loretta Haroian, were also included.

Sorensen and his research team used questionnaires with a national probability sample of 13- to 19-year-olds that conformed closely with the 1970 census figures on adolescents in terms of the numbers in each age range and in distribution by race. Their sample also reflected the national census in terms of geographic distribution and other features, such as parental income and religious background. Hass, on the other hand, limited his study geographically to Southern California. He maintains, however, that

---

*A recent book, *Alfred Kinsey: A Public/Private Life*, by James H. Jones (New York: Norton, 1997), provides some insight into problems associated with the Kinsey team's research. Despite the shortcomings of some of the work of Kinsey and his colleagues, shortcomings Kinsey himself readily admitted, the degree to which many of their findings were consistent with data reported in later studies is really quite remarkable.

his questionnaire-completing sample of 625 teenagers between the ages of 15 and 18 was comparable to any other sample that might be taken from other parts of the United States, noting, "The sexual attitudes, concerns, and activities of teenagers seem to be much more a function of a developmental period than of geographical location" (p. 123). While Hass' method of gathering volunteers (often involving direct approach at teenager-frequented localities) seemed far less satisfactory than Sorensen's technique of using a national survey research organization for area probability sampling, the close correlation of their results would tend to support Hass' assumption. The studies of Sorensen and Hass provided the bulk of the comparative portion of my own research.

Despite the fact that prep school students are viewed as having features that distinguish them from other subsets of adolescents, a computer scan of the international literature on adolescent sexuality revealed no research directly related to them. In one sense, I found this discouraging; but I confess that at the same time it was exciting to think that my study might serve to draw attention to a previously neglected area of research.

Problems

Especially in such a complex social science field as sexology, one difficulty in comparing data from different investigators lies in the use of ambiguous language. When Aaron Hass cites Kinsey as saying that 3% of women have lost their virginity "by the age of sixteen," does this mean the 16th birthday or at some point during the 16th year? The difference is not an insignificant one because, according to Hass, "Sorensen reported that 30 percent of the females . . . had engaged in sexual intercourse before the age of sixteen," and Hass himself reports 31%. My study revealed a figure of 25.6% if the expression "by the age of sixteen" means, literally, before the 16th birthday. On the other hand, if the sixteenth year of life is included, the figure jumps significantly to 54.2%, a result that squares nicely with another research-based study that reports the mean age of "loss of virginity" in urban females to be 16.2 years (Vener and Stewart 1974). Kinsey and his colleagues dealt with this problem of interpretation specifically in *Sexual Behavior in the Human Male*. They pointed out that in their sample persons from lower socioeconomic levels often calculated their ages in terms of forthcoming birthdays, the better-educated in terms of their age at their last birthday, while middle-class persons were apt to express their ages in terms of their nearest birthday, as do insurance companies. Equally important, they cite research showing that this variable is rarely accounted for in the literature of the social sciences. For consistency, therefore, the Kinsey team elected, whenever possible, to determine the precise date of birth and to calculate all ages from the past birthday.

I also encountered difficulties comparing data from various secondary sources when it came to citation verification. One example will suffice. A widely used textbook in human sexuality cites "Kinsey et al." as providing evidence that 6% of females "had had sexual intercourse by the age of thirteen" (Francoeur 1984). Yet "Kinsey et al." actually report that only *3%* percent of the females in their total sample had coital experience by *15* years of age. Clearly the two reports are incompatible. I therefore decided that, whenever possible, my research would be based on comparisons with data as reported in original sources.

Another interesting phenomenon I encountered was what appears to be observer bias. For example, in dealing with the issue of the number of different sexual partners, Hass states that his results comparing males and females "confirm those of other surveys," showing that "Girls are much less likely than boys to have engaged in sexual intercourse with many different partners." Yet, despite his use of the plural, only one such survey is actually cited and his own data, given in tabular form on the same page as this statement, contradict it; the number of females having intercourse with one to five partners is significantly *higher* than for males, both from the ages 15 to 16 and 17 to 18 (though it *is* lower when it comes to having intercourse with more than 10 partners). There are, of course, definitional problems with the word "many." Yet one cannot help but wonder if Hass' failure to notice what is at least a mild contradiction here may be related to his being tied to a male perspective of female sexuality. Such male bias *has* been noted in such fields as primatology, anthropology, and psychology.

Yet another difficulty I encountered in comparing data from different investigators is the time factor. The behavior of humans often is extremely sensitive to such influences as the social, cultural, political, or religious environment in which it develops. The influence of these factors, in turn, are themselves quite different from century to century or even decade to decade. While in the biological sciences the results yielded by identical experiments on, say, DNA-RNA transcription will yield the same data whether performed in the 1960s or 1990s (though the interpretation of these data may vary), the same cannot be said with certainty for a work of this nature. For example, when, according to Hass, Kinsey and his colleagues report that only 3% of females had "lost their virginity" by the time they were 16 but Sorensen reports a number that is tenfold higher, this does not necessarily mean that either team of investigators was at fault in their research design. Rather, other than the aforementioned ambiguity concerning age determination, the difference may simply reflect the more sexually permissive atmosphere of the 1970s when the Sorensen research was carried out as compared to the conservative 1940s and 1950s when the Kinsey team did their work. Perhaps also, in the politically conservative climate of the 1950s, women felt less able to admit the loss of their virginity than those in the 1970s, thereby preventing a more accurate result being obtained in the earlier study.

Methodology

Delimitations. With the exception of the Emma Willard School in Troy, New York, the study's sample of prep school students was limited to those who attended college preparatory schools located in New England. For the most part, for historical reasons, New England is the center for high-quality college preparatory schools. Institutions such as Choate-Rosemary Hall, Deerfield,

Groton, Phillips Andover, Phillips Exeter, St. Paul's, and so on, have for many years set a standard for academic excellence that all other prep schools attempt to emulate. Thus my assumption was that, if one is going to study the prep school world, it makes sense to seek out those institutions that best exemplify that world. Despite some notable exceptions, such as The Hill School in Pennsylvania and Lawrenceville in New Jersey, such schools are found in New England.

The sample of public school graduates had matriculated at the same colleges and universities as had the prep school student sample and had therefore met a range of college admission standards comparable to those encountered by the graduates of the college preparatory schools with whom they were being compared.

Research Instrument. With the aid of my dissertation committee and others, I developed a questionnaire as the principal research instrument. While most of the questions were appropriate for both sexes, separate questionnaires were designed for females and males with sections of gender-specific questions. Both female and male questionnaires also contained a section with questions appropriate only for preparatory school students, such as questions concerning dormitory life. The questionnaires contained between 197 and 234 items, depending on the sex of the respondent and the type of school attended. Trial runs with six volunteer students allowed for some minor revisions for face validity and revealed that the time required to complete the questionnaire was approximately 30 minutes (134 of the items possessed only one degree of freedom, that is, they required only a "yes/no" or "true/false" response), the maximum time reported as being effective.

Many of the questionnaire items were selected to allow for comparisons between the results of this study and those of earlier investigators, especially Sorensen and Hass. Where appropriate, the same questionnaire items were used. In other instances, I edited items for clarification, for example, to eliminate 1970s slang that might not be meaningful to an 18-year-old in the

1980s. The questionnaire also asked for volunteers to be interviewed. I felt that these interviews might provide further information about the schools that would be helpful in accounting for
differences between the experimental and control groups should
any differences be found. No attempts at reliability or validity
measures were made in compiling the interviews.

The Sample. To obtain a reasonable degree of uniformity in
scholastic ability yet still ensure a sample that was representative
of U.S. college-bound teens, the sample students were those who
had been accepted into the same colleges and universities and
thus had met the admission standards set by those institutions.
The students were contacted directly, either immediately after
graduation from their secondary school or on the college campuses. This technique ensured that their secondary school experiences were fresh in their minds and eliminated the need for
obtaining school or parent permission. The latter factor is especially important because — though Sorensen found otherwise —
some might argue that a sample of students whose parents are
likely to give permission might arguably be said to represent a
more liberal, and thus atypical, segment of the population.

This last point deserves amplification in terms of the sample
size. According to Kinsey, "the volunteers who make up the partial sample may represent a more active group of individuals, of
the type which is aggressive, responds to a call for cooperation in
a survey, and is more responsive and less inhibited sexually. It is
true that the last persons to contribute in a hundred percent sample are sometimes the more prudish, restrained, apathetic, and
sexually less active individual" (1948, p. 102). Those not responding to my surveys may well have been of that persuasion,
thus limiting the sample size. Kinsey also stated that "the persons
contributing to the hundred percent sample may have covered up
more of the fact, because they did not contribute as willingly as
the volunteers who made up the partial sample" (p. 103). My partial sample dealt with willing volunteers. Kinsey maintained that
"hundred percent samples are of smaller size than the partial

samples, and therefore less reliable. The partial samples show wider ranges of variation, and this raises the values of the means. With larger series, the means in the hundred percent samples might be raised. . . . The above comparisons indicated that there is considerable merit to samples obtained from volunteers who respond to a general appeal for histories." It should be kept in mind, however, that the three and a half decades separating this study from that of Kinsey and his colleagues may make these concerns less applicable here.

The 16 private schools involved in the study were selected because of their preeminence in the prep school world and their accessibility. Student directories identifying seniors and providing their home addresses were obtained either directly from the schools or from individual administrators, faculty members, or students interested in having their school included in the study. In the case of large schools, with some 185 to 350 graduating seniors, one senior in five was sampled; in the case of the smaller schools, with graduating classes of fewer than 100, one senior in three was sampled. The sample students were sent letters requesting their participation in the study and assuring anonymity and thus confidentiality. Each letter was coded so that the school attended by the student could be identified. As soon as positive responses were obtained, questionnaires appropriate to the responder's gender were sent out, along with an accompanying letter of instructions. A self-addressed, postage-paid envelope was provided for returning the questionnaire.

The return percentage of the volunteer letter was 38.6%. Of these, 84.3% completed and returned the questionnaire. Of those who responded to the survey, 37.1% volunteered to be interviewed. Several wrote notes requesting to see the results of the study and asking if they could be of further help. The comparable number of public school students volunteering for interviews was 30%.

The public school sample was obtained in a different manner. At Wesleyan University, a form letter was sent to all of the public and prep school graduates among the university's 650 first-year students. Each letter was addressed to the student by his or her name and campus post office box number. I decided to delay the mailing until three days after the traditional orientation week for first-year students, because during that week students are deluged with mail competing for their time and attention. At the same time, I recognized that too long a delay would provide more time for the students to get to know each other and thus increase the likelihood of sharing information or even working together on the questionnaires. The fact that all of the sampling was completed within less than eight days after the students arrived on campus increased the confidence level that little, if any, such sharing was done.

On the day of the distribution of the letter into the first-year students' mailboxes, one or more assistants and I were present just outside the post office door, with a sign identifying us, in order to reinforce the volunteer-requesting letter's message and provide the questionnaire immediately. Because I had access to faculty services, an interoffice, self-addressed envelope was provided for returning the surveys. The process was repeated at the post office the following day for students who had not yet visited their mailboxes and, later, at the entryway to the dining hall where all first-year students eat. Similar procedures were followed at two public universities, University of Virginia and Southern Connecticut University, with procedural variations depending mostly on the institutions' policies regarding such matters and campus geography with regard to the best way of contacting first-year students.

Demographics. Because of the nature of this study, the possibility of obtaining a random sample comparable to Sorensen's was precluded. The mean age of the study sample was 18.6 years. All were college-bound. They were predominantly white (95.5%). Only 2.6% identified themselves as being from a poverty-level income bracket, with 50.2% self-identifying with a moderate income level and 47.2% an upper income level. Approximately one-fourth (26.6%) came from families in which the parents were divorced. Concerning religious background, 23% identified themselves as Roman Catholic, 20.8% as Jewish, and 39.4% as Protestant, with the remainder coming mostly from agnostic or atheistic environments. These demographic data refer specifically to the religious environment in which the sample persons were raised as children and not to their current religious views, which, on the whole, seemed to be more liberal than those of their parents. The same shift in attitudes was identifiable in the respondents' political views, which also generally tended to be more liberal than those of their parents.

In order to ascertain if the sample was representative of the overall student populations of the colleges attended, demographic information was obtained from the three universities, Wesleyan, University of Virginia, and Southern Connecticut University. There were two areas in which direct comparisons were possible: religious background and ethnic origin. Of the college population, 42.5% were Protestant compared to 39.4% of the sample; 22% were Jewish compared to 20.8% of the sample; and 22.5% were Roman Catholic compared to 23% of the sample. Thirteen percent were categorized as "other" (that is, Islamic, agnostic, atheist, etc.) compared to 17.8% of the sample. Ethnically, 85% of the college population was white, 8.5% black, and 6.5% represented other ethnic minorities, such as Hispanics, Asians, and so forth. The study sample contained 94.5% white and 3.5% black respondents, with 2% other minorities.

Treatment of Data and Statistics. The null hypothesis was that there would be *no* difference between the experimental and control group (represented by the public school students). This technique was chosen because, as William C. Schefler writes:

> If we state our hypothesis in the null form, our objective is then to statistically reject it, thus lending support to the claim that a significant difference is involved. Note the absence of the "prove" in the preceding statement. The use of the null hypothesis is logically sound. . . . No matter how much evidence is gathered in support of a specific hypothesis, one can never be certain that this same body of evidence

would not equally support any number of unknown alternative hypotheses! On the other hand, it is logically possible to reject a hypothesis, since this can be done by finding evidence which contradicts it. (1979, p. 55)

In order to facilitate access to desired comparison data I chose the computer program, Statistical Conversion for the Social Sciences (SCSS), a variation of the Statistical Package for the Social Sciences (SPSS). SCSS allows for a wide range of statistical techniques and for greater focus on the research itself, rather than on computer coding language techniques. The data transformation facilities of SCSS permit the generation of new variables, the revision of the values of existing variables, additions to or alteration of variable and value labels, application and removal of missing value indicators, and the sampling, selection, or weighing of the data (Sours 1982). The SCSS system provides for maximum flexibility within the overall research design, quickly providing answers to questions that arise in a wide variety of "dialects," ranging from descriptive statistics, simple frequency distributions with histograms, cross-tabulations, simple correlations, partial correlations, means and variances for sub-populations, T tests, scatter plots, stepwise multiple regression with analysis of residuals, and factor analysis — far more versatility, in fact, than this or any other research study of this sort actually requires. It is the fact that SCSS allows one to proceed naturally through data analysis, asking questions as they arise and basing further questions on the answers received, that is its most helpful feature.

Data collected through the questionnaires were entered into the DECSYSTEM-20 computer facilities of Wesleyan University. Various types of data analyses were performed (for example, frequency distribution, cross-tabulations, and so on). From these statistics, data could be generated, if desired, concerning mean, median, mode and range, and, of course, probability data based on the chi square analysis. In accordance with generally accepted social science research practice, the levels of significance were based on chi square values indicating significance at the 0.05 level. All percentages calculated were adjusted to allow for missing values. In computing the chi square according to the standard formula, I noted that there is some disagreement in the statistics literature concerning the use of the Yates correction factor — the subtraction of 0.50 from the absolute difference between each observed and expected frequency combination for one degree of freedom ("yes/no," or "true/false" questions). Such questions could be organized in the form of a 2 x 2 table, with the percentage of "true/yes" and "false/no" responses along the x axis crossed by "observed" and "expected" on the y axis.

In the case of questionnaire items with one degree of freedom, Schefler states that "it would be well to use the Yates correction factor for *all* 2 x 2 table situations, regardless of the size of cell values" (p. 88). However, disagreement with this view was expressed by one of my statistical advisors, who felt that its use in this study would be superfluous. In order to resolve the issue, calculations using the Yates correction factor were performed on a random sample of questionnaire items (from my study and Sorensen's) with one degree of freedom. The results bore out my advisor's contention: The operation made no statistically significant difference.

I recognized that the chi square analysis, despite its widespread use, is not a good measure of association between two variables unless adjustments are made for differences in sample size and degrees of freedom, as well as to restrict the range of values to those between zero and one. This is done by use of the phi-coefficient, which divides the chi square by the sample size and the coefficient of contingency to adjust for tables in which one of the dimensions is greater than two. However, in this study, the sample sizes being compared were within a range which made such adjustments unnecessary.

Phase One: Comparison with Sorensen

The sample in my study was first compared with that used by the team of researchers headed by Robert Sorensen: a national probability sample of U.S. teenagers. I did this to determine if my

sample (the prep school and college-bound public school students combined) differed in any significant way from the larger
Sorensen sample. The comparison involved responses of 38 questionnaire items that were identical in both studies. These 38 items
possessed only one degree of freedom. My reasoning was that if
no significant differences were found, then this would indicate
that whatever differences there might be between my prep school
student sample and Sorensen's sample, composed almost entirely
of college-bound and non-college-bound public school students,
they were not powerful enough to overcome being subjected to a
sort of "swamping effect" of the college-bound public school students in my sample. Thus differences, if any existed, could only
be detected by a comparative analysis within my study sample
itself — that is, by comparing prep school students with their college-bound public school counterparts. On the other hand, if differences *were* found when compared to Sorensen's sample, the
nature of these differences would provide cues for the creation of
hypotheses to account for these differences.

Before carrying out this direct comparison to the Sorensen
research team's data, I confirmed that the sample of this study
was not atypical in the more biological aspects of sexuality; for
example, in age of first menstruation (though even this seemingly strictly biological factor is well known to be influenced by such
environmental inputs as the availability of the proper food and
sociocultural influences, for example, rural versus industrial living). The mean age of first menstruation of the study sample was
12.78, a figure that fell well within the range of 11 to 13 years
given by many sources and matched almost exactly the mean age
of 12.8 cited by Francoeur (1984). Likewise, the range of ages for
first masturbation for the majority of males fell within the range
of 12 to 17 years of age given by Kinsey. Finally, the mean age
of first intercourse for both males and females in the sample was
16.04, a figure comparable with data provided elsewhere. For
example, Kantner and Zelnik (1979) report a mean age of 16.2
for urban females, while Kirkendall (1968) gives a mean age of
17.1 for both females and males. Indeed, the mean age range for

first intercourse may well be rather uniform throughout Western culture; Caletti (1978), for example, reports a range of 15–18 years for Italian females and males.

The null hypothesis, predicting no significant differences between my total sample and Sorensen's total sample, was refuted. A comparison of responses to 38 Sorensen questionnaire items revealed significant differences on 74% of them. My first hypothesis to account for these differences was that the presence of the prep school students was the causative factor. Accordingly, I decided to remove the prep school student data from my sample (thus leaving only the college-bound public school respondents) and again make the comparison with Sorensen's total sample. The results did not support my "preppie hypothesis." Of the 28 questions that previously showed significant differences, only three changed from "significant" to "not significant" — though, interestingly, two questions, dealing with drugs and sex, moved in the other direction, from "not significant" to "significant."

Another variable that might be causing the disparity was age. As I noted earlier, Sorensen's sample ranged from 13 to 19 years of age while mine was composed almost entirely of 18-year-olds. Unfortunately, it was not possible to use all of the 38 previously used questionnaire items in order to test a hypothesis proposing age as the causative factor because Sorensen did not break down his subject pool into ages. However, for 19 of the 38 items in which the narrower age range of 16 to 19 *is* given, significant differences were still found on 17 items. Thus my "age hypothesis" also was refuted.

My last resort was to put forth a hypothesis proposing that the high percentage of significant differences between my sample and that of Sorensen was because of the former's atypical nature, being composed entirely of college-bound students. In order to test this hypothesis, the 28 questionnaire items on which significant differences were found between my sample and Sorensen's were compared. The "college-bound" hypothesis predicts that such a comparison should produce a considerable reduction in the number of significant differences between the two groups.

The results supported this hypothesis, or at the very least were consistent with it; of the 28 items, significant differences remained in only 10 of them.

Based on these preliminary studies, it seemed obvious to me that the most meaningful comparison for my study would be one between the prep school graduates of my sample and their closest public school counterparts, that is, those public school graduates who were either attending college or who were planning to attend. These were precisely the public school students who composed that portion of my sample. The comparison was carried out by selecting topics in sexuality that possess both behavioral and attitudinal aspects and including items in the questionnaire (usually separated from each other) that would detect these. For example, questions were designed both to reveal if the respondents had had sexual intercourse and how they felt about premarital sexual intercourse in general. Similarly, other questions asked if the respondents had had any experience with prostitutes and then how they felt about laws against prostitution.

Phase Two: The Null Hypothesis

As in my comparison with Sorensen, my strategy for the main focus of my study involved using the null hypothesis that there is no significant difference between the sexual attitudes and behavior of prep school and public school students. For purposes of simplification, I decided to divide the 15 areas of comparison into three categories: behavioral, biological, and attitudinal. The boundaries between these groupings are somewhat arbitrary, because there are behavioral, biological, and attitudinal aspects to all 15. Nonetheless, the groupings proved to be useful. They are shown in Table 1.

A word might be said about the inclusion of masturbation and homosexuality under the heading "biological," because these involve behavioral acts generally associated with strong attitudinal features as well. Indeed, it will be noted that homosexuality also appears under the "attitudinal" heading, because significant

Table 1. Categories used for comparisons, with significant differences indicated.

Behavioral	Biological	Attitudinal
Virginity*	Orgasm	Homosexuality*
Oral - genital sex*	Masturbation	Drugs and sex*
Birth control, abortion	Pregnancy	Incest*
Anal sex, bestiality, and sadomasochism*	Homosexuality	Prostitution*
	Sexually transmitted diseases	Pornography*
Drugs and sex*	Incest	Monogamy*
Incest*		Religion and sex*
Prostitution		Politics and gender*
Pornograpy		
Monogamy		
*Significant difference > 0.05		

differences in attitudes toward homosexuality appeared here. Nonetheless, due perhaps to my background in biology, I would argue that, regardless of what cultural views may have been imposed on us, both masturbation and same-sex sexual interactions are natural biological phenomena, widely spread throughout the animal kingdom and, especially in the case of masturbation, may play an important role in the development of the range of biological behaviors we term "sexual." The word *development* in the last sentence is a critical one. Biology and psychology now recognize that behavior is no less subject to developmental processes than the growth of any purely anatomical structure. This point is one to which considerable attention must be paid by any individual or institution genuinely interested in the nature of the education process.

The inclusion of incest in all three categories was simply to avoid giving the impression of favoring an either/or cultural versus biological basis for the incest taboo. Harvard University biologist E.O. Wilson (1975) and others have argued that the avoidance of inbreeding may be the result of natural selection operating on the genome to favor such avoidance. Others, of the B.F. Skinner or Levi-Strauss schools of thought, argue strongly for a mostly environmental or cultural basis for incest avoidance. Neither of the two items in my questionnaire dealing with incest could provide any information bearing on this matter, and so my inclusion of incest under all three headings was merely to avoid giving the impression of favoring one view over the other.

Monogamy appears under "behavioral," despite the fact that no significant behavioral differences were found. Indeed, one might use this fact to argue that monogamy in humans should be classified as a biologically based phenomenon. Unfortunately, to do so would be to fly in the face of vast amounts of sociological, anthropological, and biological data. Concerning the last, for example, with the possible exception of the gibbon, the order Primata (to which *Homo sapiens* belongs) is essentially non-monogamous, with our closest relative, the chimpanzee, notoriously so in both males and females. It seems clear, therefore, that at least in principle monogamy in humans is culturally imposed, rather than a biological imperative. One can only guess that the uniformity of behavior of the prep school and public school students in my sample concerning monogamy (which, interestingly, often is at variance with their attitudes concerning it) merely represents the degree to which this form of behavior is stressed and legally enforced in our society. Other categories also appear in more than one column, either in recognition of their complex nature or because of the results obtained. By constituting the categories in this manner, it became immediately obvious that, in the biological aspects of their sexual behavior, college preparatory students and public school students are virtually identical. It is only in the areas of behavior and attitudes that significant differences are found. I shall deal with the behavioral differences first.

Behavioral Differences. The areas in which statistically significant behavioral differences were found between the prep school and public school students in my sample may be summarized as follows:

- Virginity: Prep school males and females reported a significantly higher "loss of virginity" than did their public school counterparts.

- Sexual experimentation: The prep school students appeared to be considerably more sophisticated in their range of sexual experimentation (for example, cunnilingus, fellatio, and so on) than did the public school students.

- Drugs and sex: Both prep school males and females reported having sex under the influence of drugs with someone they ordinarily would not have sex with to an extent that was highly significant (> 0.001) when compared to public school males and females. A significantly greater number of prep school females reported having engaged in sexual activities that they would not ordinarily have engaged in if it had not been for their use of drugs.

- Incest: A significantly higher percentage of prep school males reported sexual contact with a relative than did public school males.

Because the occurrence of incest in either group was not a major part of this study, I will comment on it only briefly. The significantly higher incidence of incestual relations reported by prep school males than prep school females is at variance with most of the literature, which generally reports that incest with female children or adolescents is more common than with male children or adolescents. However, the only two items dealing with incest do not reveal what sort of incest was involved (brother-sister, father-daughter, mother-son, or between two related individuals of the same sex). Thus, at least in terms of behavior, the instances in question may be simply cases of "playing doctor" and the differences due only to a greater unwillingness on the part of females to reveal this, even on an anonymous questionnaire. Such hypotheses may be tested only by using questions designed to ferret out critical information that I did not deem germane for the purposes of my investigation.

Attitudinal Differences. The attitudinal differences between the prep school students and college-bound public school students in my sample may be summarized as follows:

- Homosexuality: A significantly larger number of prep school males than public school males ruled out ever having a homosexual experience and significantly more prep school males labeled homosexuality abnormal than did public school males.

- Drugs and sex: A highly significant (> 0.001) number of prep school males reported seeing nothing wrong in taking sexual advantage of someone under the influence of drugs.

- Incest: A significantly higher number of prep school males disapproved of sexual interaction between a parent and a child than did public school males.

- Prostitution: A significantly higher number of prep school females felt that both the prostitute and the customer should be punished than did public school females.

- Pornography: The prep school sample felt significantly less guilt viewing pornographic materials. Yet a significantly greater number of prep school females felt it should be against the law for people to read about or to see certain sexual acts, and a significantly greater number of prep school males reported feeling that pornography was harmful to certain kinds of people than did public school males.

- Monogamy: Prep school males, and for the most part prep school females, were significantly more tolerant of having several sex partners and extramarital sex than were public school males and females.

- Religion and sex: A highly significant (> 0.001) number of prep school males denied that God was interested in their sexual behavior as compared with public school males.

- Politics and gender: A significantly lower number of prep school males and females were supportive of equal rights for both sexes.

The attitudes of my sample students concerning incest, prostitution, and pornography were of only minor interest to my study and thus will be dealt with only very briefly. Their main significance lies in the fact that, as was the case in other areas, they reveal a wide discrepancy between prep school students' attitudes concerning sex and sexuality and their actual behavior. For example, the amount of reading of pornographic materials was virtually identical for both prep and public school students. Yet, as I noted in Chapter 7, while prep school students reported reading pornography with significantly less personal guilt than did the public school students, they would still restrict access to these materials to others. Similarly, prep school males reported a significantly higher degree of incestual relations than did public school males, but they also were significantly more condemning of such activities than their public school counterparts. (It is interesting to note that Sorensen found the reverse in his mostly public school sample. His respondents tolerated sexual behavior for others that they did not necessarily tolerate in themselves.) Clearly, there is a strong element of intellectual elitism here and, as I stressed previously, prep schools have historically represented an elitist class. Such elitism also has been suggested to account for brother-sister incest among the wealthy. Justice and Justice (1979) coined the term "elitist incestuous relationship" for such activity and suggested that it is based on the idea that the rich consider themselves far too good to carry out such activity with the rest of the world.

Concerning prostitution, only one significant attitudinal difference appeared between the prep school and public school samples. Through an oversight, however, while questions were asked about whether the law should punish the prostitute and not the customer, the customer and not the prostitute, or both the prostitute and the customer, no question allowed for the choice of no punishment at all. This unfortunate omission makes any conclusions tenuous. What emerged quite clearly, however, was yet another seeming dichotomy between behavior and attitudes. While only males reported visiting prostitutes, a highly signifi-

cant number (> 0.005) would punish the prostitute and not the
customer than would females.

Results Summary

Following is a summary of the results of my study comparing
the sexual behavior and attitudes of New England prep school
students to their closest public school counterparts. For simplici-
ty, the use of the word "significant" in the material which follows
is limited to those comparisons in which the differences were
greater than the generally accepted 0.05.

Virginity. The percent of nonvirgins overall was significantly
higher among prep school students (66.4%) than public (47.5%),
with the difference between prep and public school males being
greater than between prep and public school females. The total
number of different sexual partners also was much higher among
private school students, though more public than prep school
students reported having more than 10 partners.

Both groups reported feeling glad they had had sexual intercourse when they did. Yet, when responding to a question
containing a list of words to choose among describing the experience — examples: "happy," "sad," "joyful," "raped," "sorry,"
"guilty," and so on — only 59% of the prep school students
selected highly positive terms and only 48.9% of the public
school students did so. Indeed, fully one-quarter of the public
school students selected negative terms compared to only about
one-eighth of the prep school students.

Orgasm. The attainment of orgasm during sexual intercourse
presents a mixed picture. Overall, 45.8% of prep school graduates reported orgasm 100% of the time compared to only 30% of
the public school graduates. Among females, however, note that
the numbers were reversed and far lower, with only 3.2% of the
prep school females reporting orgasm 100% of the time compared to 11.1% of the public school females. In males, the figures
were 78% for prep school males and 69.2% for public school

males. Yet more prep school females reported being multi-orgasmic (42.5%) than those from public schools (35.5%). The male figures for many orgasms were 53.3% and 26.3%, respectively, a difference significant to the 0.001 level. Considered altogether, however, the differences between the two groups were not statistically significant.

Oral-Genital Sex. The amount of reported oral-genital sexual activity was significantly greater among prep school students than among public school students. For example, 77.9% of prep school females had experienced cunnilingus as opposed to only 60% of the public school females, while the incidence of performing fellatio was 67.6% for prep school female and 58.3% for the public school female. Concerning overall heterosexual oral-genital activity, the prep school percentages were significantly higher. No questions were asked to determine the amount of oral-genital activity between males or between females. A large percentage of both groups reported enjoyment of oral-genital contact, both giving and receiving, with males enjoying it more than females. Only one student (prep school) in the entire sample indicated that religious teachings would prevent him from participating in oral-genital sexual contact. By contrast 98% of the prep school students and 96% of the public school students rejected the view taught by some religious denominations that such contact is "abnormal" or "unnatural."

Masturbation. Responses to the question, "If you have masturbated, how old do you estimate you were when you first masturbated to orgasm?" revealed a mean age of 12.78 for both groups, although only 68.5% responded. The difference between prep school and public school students was not significant; in both groups females reported a later age. The vast majority disagreed with a questionnaire item quoting a 1977 Vatican statement labeling masturbation as "a grave moral disorder" and "an intrinsically disordered act," while an even larger percentage of the prep school and public school respondents marked as "false" the item, "I would not masturbate *because it is against my religion.*"

Birth Control, Pregnancy, and Abortion. Both sample groups showed remarkable uniformity concerning their views of birth control and abortion. For example, 57.9% of the prep school students and 60.4% of the public school students indicated they would not have sexual intercourse without using a contraceptive, and 81.7% of the prep school students and 83.9% of the public school students said they always inquired if the partner was using a contraceptive before intercourse.

One hundred percent of both groups marked "false" the statement, "I would not practice birth control *because it is against my religion*," despite the fact that almost one fourth (23%) of the total sample identified themselves as Roman Catholic. Perhaps still more interesting is that 99.2% of the prep school graduates and 89.5% of the public school graduates believed birth control should be made available to teenagers without their parents' consent, and the proportion opposing the "Right-to-Life" proposal for a constitutional amendment outlawing abortion was approximately the same. However, about one-half of prep and public school females reported that they would feel guilty about having an abortion.

Only three of the prep school females had been pregnant, and all elected to have abortions. Three public school females had been pregnant, with one getting married and keeping the infant, one having an abortion, and one miscarrying.

Homosexuality. Both groups estimated that about 10% of their secondary school classmates had had sexual experience with someone of the same gender, with prep school females giving a slightly higher estimate than did their public school counterparts. A similar estimate of 10% was given for the proportion of gay and lesbian faculty, with again a slightly higher percentage in the prep schools. Concerning personal homosexual experiences, the slightly higher 13.3% reported by prep school males compared to 10% reported by public school males was counterbalanced by a 7.5% figure reported by prep school females in comparison to 10.5% reported by their public school counterparts.

The preceding data, however, merely reveal the percent who reported having had a homosexual experience and not the percent who self-identified as *gay* or *lesbian*. A questionnaire item described the Kinsey scale of sexual orientation and then asked the respondents to circle the number that most closely identified their own self-perceived sexual orientation. The results were that 59.4% of the prep school students and 55.4% of the public school students circled 0, completely heterosexual. Only 1% of the public school sample circled 6, completely homosexual, and another 1% circled 5, while no private school students circled 6 and only 8% circled 4 or 5. More prep school students ruled out ever having a homosexual experience than did public school students. While the females showed slightly more openness concerning this possibility, again the prep school females lagged behind the public school females in this regard. Consistent with these data are those showing that a higher percentage of prep school students perceived homosexuality as "abnormal" than did the public school students, and both groups admitted that a known homosexual would not be treated with respect at their schools. With all of the preceding in mind, it is interesting to note that, despite the reservations about homosexuality expressed by the respondents (which another questionnaire item revealed they blame mostly on their peers), a large majority of both prep school and public school students checked "true" to an item, "It is ethically or morally wrong for a religious organization to refuse to accept homosexuals into the ministry."

Sexually Transmitted Diseases. Only one prep school female reported having herpes, with one prep school male, when asked to choose between gonorrhea, herpes, syphilis, and "other," selected "other." In the public school sample, 2.5% of the males reported having gonorrhea and 1.7% of the females herpes. Avoidance of sexual contact because of fear of venereal disease was reported by 9.1% and 9.5% of the total prep and public school samples, respectively, with the males of both groups reporting a greater fear than did females.

Anal Sex, Bestiality, and Sadomasochism. The questionnaire item, "Have you engaged in anal intercourse?" revealed that significantly more prep school males had done so than had public school males, while the differences reported by prep and public school females were not significant. The item asking, "Have you ever had sexual contact with an animal?" again revealed a significantly higher amount of prep school males than public school males responding affirmatively, but there were no significant differences between the females.

No item asked directly about participation in sexual sadomasochism. However, five true-false questions related to this theme were asked.

Drugs and Sex. While the amount of alcohol consumption reported in their homes showed no significant differences between prep school and public school students, the on-campus consumption of alcohol was higher at prep schools, possibly because for the prep school boarder the school is a 24-hour-a-day, home-away-from-home environment during the academic year. It is in the use of drugs in conjunction with sex, however, that the differences between the two groups becomes highly significant (> 0.001). One item asked, "Have you ever had sex under the influence of drugs with a person with whom you would not ordinarily have had sex?" The percent of prep school graduates responding affirmatively was more than twice that of their public school counterparts. The largest difference was between the prep school and public school females. This same result was noted in the response to the item asking, "Have you ever engaged in a sexual activity that you would not have if you had not taken the drug?" While here the prep school males were slightly lower in an affirmative response than public school males, the prep school females remained significantly higher than their public school counterparts. The responses to the item asking, "Do you feel it would be wrong to take advantage of a person who was under the influence of a drug or drugs by having sex with that person?" were equally interesting and, for the males, statistically significant, with far more prep school males than public school males seeing nothing wrong with it.

Incest. The incest taboo held true for both groups. Incest was disapproved of, even if voluntary, by a large majority of both prep and public school graduates, with the females of both groups rating it less acceptable than did males. In both groups, the differences in actual reported incidence of sexual activity with a relative were not significant, being only slightly higher for public school students; but the figures for males were significantly higher than for females.

Prostitution. None of the females in the sample had paid for sex, while 5.1% of the males had done so. Concerning law enforcement, three questions asked if the law should punish the prostitute, not the customer; the customer, not the prostitute; or both. Some 57.4% prep and 52.2% public school graduates thought both should be punished, but still more felt the prostitute was guiltier than the customer, with more males than females in both groups condemning the prostitute. Though the overall difference was not statistically significant, especially interesting was the reaction to an item based on the medieval church practice, still occasionally found today, concerning "unnatural" sex acts and the role of prostitutes in "keeping the marriage bed holy" (Valentini and di Meglio 1975). This item, "I believe that it is better for a male to go to a female prostitute than to engage in sex with his wife in a manner that violates the teachings of some religions," received a "true" from 9.1% of prep school males and 8.3% from public school males, while 7.4% of the prep school females and 12% of the public school females responded affirmatively.

Pornography. The question dealing with pornography yielded results that were interesting not because of any significant differences between the two groups but for the disparity they revealed between behavior and attitudes. Approximately three out of four prep and public school males admitted having obtained pornography; among females, slightly less than half had done so. Only

8.1% of prep school and 13.8% of public school graduates felt that it was "abnormal" to be sexually aroused by pornography, while only 17.4% of prep school and 29.2% of public school graduates confessed to feeling guilty while reading or seeing pornographic materials. Similar proportions of responses occurred with the item, "I think it should be against the law for people to read about or see certain sexual acts." It also was interesting to note that 20% and 29%, respectively, of prep school and public school males believed that their parents either owned pornographic material or went to see pornographic films, and 10.8% and 16.4%, respectively, of the females believed so. Despite these responses, a large percentage of the prep school and public school males believed that "pornography is harmful to certain kinds of people in our society," and still larger percentages of the prep and public school females believed so.

Monogamy. Both groups held similar views concerning the advisability of having several sex partners, with only an insignificant trace of a double standard being detectable. However, the questions made it explicit that this experimentation preceded "settling down with one." During the "experimental" period, 35.6% of prep and 33% of public school students wanted many partners, with females expressing this desire more than males, but it was meant in terms of a sort of "serial monogamy," rather than having sex with more than one at the same time. Only a small percentage of the prep school and public school sample had experienced group sex. This conservatism continued when it came to having sex with another partner after a "going steady" relationship had been established. It is interesting to note that prep school females were three times more "liberal" than their male counterparts on this matter, but the situation was reversed among the public school respondents.

When it came to opinions on extramarital sexual relations, this conservative attitude continued. Questions dealing with opinions on extramarital affairs for the wife and husband, respectively, brought negative responses higher than 90% from both groups, with again only an insignificant trace of a double standard. Furthermore, an item that asked for opinions on extramarital sex, on a scale of one to ten, again brought forth strong disapproval. However, in terms of actually divorcing the "unfaithful" spouse, only about one-fourth of both groups indicated that they would do so.

Religion and Sex. The item stating, "I believe that God is interested in my sexual behavior," a positive variation of the same question asked by Sorensen, received a negative response from approximately three-fourths of the prep school and public school graduates, the difference between the two groups not being statistically significant except in the case of the prep and public school males' still more negative response.

Politics and Gender. One item instructed respondents, "On a scale of 1 to 10, rate your feelings about feminism and equal rights for all, regardless of gender," with a "1" response meaning "strongly supportive" and a "10" response meaning "strongly opposed." In each group females were significantly more supportive than males, and the percentages of 1s and 2s chosen by both male and female public school graduates was significantly greater than their prep school counterparts.

Testing Other Hypotheses

One of the more interesting things to do after all the data are collected, fed into the computer, and analyzed is to check previously generated hypotheses of others to see if their predictions are supported by the new data. One such hypothesis was advanced several years ago by psychologist James W. Prescott while at the National Institute of Child Health and Development. Prescott (1975) suggested that sensory deprivation during early development is a principle cause of violence. This conclusion was based on his research and the earlier work of others (most notably the classic experiments of Harry and Margaret Harlow at the University of Wisconsin on sensory deprivation in Rhesus monkeys), plus cross-cultural analyses of human societies. Prescott's hypothesis seems supported by historian Erwin J. Haeberle, who has written that "historical and cross-cultural studies show all too clearly that sexual violence and misery often spring directly from unrealistic, unreasonable, and unnecessary social regulations" (1978, p. 216). Prescott has elsewhere argued that religious teachings encouraging sensory deprivation, most especially those of a sexual nature (masturbation, physical intimacy, and so forth), are unwittingly producing individuals whose violence often spills over into such widespread social problems as spouse or child abuse, rape, or a tendency to associate sexual gratification with pain or violence. According to Prescott, conservative Catholicism, fundamentalist Protestantism, and Orthodox Judaism fall generally under this heading. Because my questionnaire identified both conservative and liberal religious upbringing and asked respondents questions to determine if they associated pain or violence with sexual feelings in their sexual fantasies, an opportunity was provided to test Prescott's hypothesis.

The best that can be said for the results is that they are merely consistent with the Prescott hypothesis. The data do show that a considerably higher percentage of public school students have such fantasies than do prep school students, and the former also show a higher percentage of religiously conservative backgrounds. However, these data do not reveal the critical information as to whether those individuals who have such fantasies actually *are* from the sort of background Prescott describes. It was possible with the statistical program I used to see if such correlation did, indeed, exist. However, because this issue was only peripherally related to my study, I elected not to do it. It would make an interesting research project, however.

More interesting to me were data related to what I elected to label the "feminist hypothesis," linking the current male dominance of our society's economic structure to the political repression of women. It is no accident, for example, that the National Organization of Women singled out corporate power and its economic interests to receive most of the blame for the defeat of the

Equal Rights Amendment, despite the fact that there were other obvious political targets (for example, the Religious Right) that might well have been selected. The feminist hypothesis, as defined here, suggests that those who possess economic advantages by reason of family income, thereby passing through their formative years in the sort of environment such advantages often bestow, might reflect "conservative views" that are unenthusiastic regarding equal rights for women. Consistent with this hypothesis is the fact that prep school graduates were significantly less supportive of "feminism and equal rights for all, regardless of gender" than were public school graduates. Not surprisingly, the prep school students reported family incomes considerably higher than those reported by public school graduates.

However, these factors in themselves are no more significant to the feminist hypothesis than were the analogous data on prep-versus-public school religious backgrounds to the Prescott hypothesis. Needed was a cross-tabulation that could determine if those public and private school students from higher-income families did, indeed, tend to be less supportive of equal rights of all regardless of gender than their lower-income peers. I therefore made cross-tabulation comparisons between the sample students on the basis of their responses to items dealing with family income, their self-described place on the political spectrum, and their feelings about feminism and equal rights for all regardless of gender. The data are supportive of the feminist hypothesis or, at the very least, consistent with it. For example, on a scale of 1 to 10, ranging from "strongly supportive" to "opposed," no one in the lower-income category selected a number greater than 2 on the scale in support of equal rights and feminism, thus placing themselves in the "strongly supportive" category. In both the middle- and upper-income categories, however, eight out of the 10 choices were selected. No one chose 9 or 10, representing strong opposition to equal rights and feminism (seemingly nobody wanted to be labeled, even anonymously, as a total reactionary). However, a slight shift toward the less-supportive end of the scale was noticeable as the income level increased, even though the overall trend for the total sample was liberal and supportive.

Of course, this may well be an example of what my husband has labeled the "bumper sticker effect." While it is common to see bumper stickers with slogans such as "Split Wood, Not Atoms," "No Nukes," and "Support the Equal Rights Amendment" on one car, and "America: Love it or Leave it," "Support the NRA," and "Abortion is Murder" on another, we would be surprised to see any slogans from the first set mixed with those in the second. Similarly, it would be surprising if those respondents who identified themselves as politically liberal were seriously opposed to equal rights for both genders, or the other way around. In brief, that there may be a correlation in one or more such areas is obvious; that there is any clear cause-and-effect is not. It also should be stressed that we are dealing with a three-variable comparison, not two, because the way the students identified themselves on the political spectrum also was included in the analysis along with income level and their feelings about gender equality. Thus by no means are these data conclusive; rather, they are suggestive. Historically, however, suggestiveness often has proven to be fruitful ground for further research.

Usefulness of the Research Technique

A final word is appropriate concerning the technique used in this study in contacting sample respondents after they had arrived on the campuses of the colleges and universities of their choice. In contrast with Hass, who reported that he found the obtaining of volunteers so difficult that he would never do such a study again,* this technique turned out to be remarkably fruitful and easy, requiring only a day or so of on-campus working time. Trying to contact the respondents while still minors and getting the permission of both the schools' administrators and parents would have been virtually impossible. Even if a sample using such a technique were obtained, its validity could be legitimately challenged.

---

*Personal communication, 1983.

The lack cited by the respondents of any involvement of religious teachings in dictating their behavior suggests that a repetition of this study substituting religiously based school students for the New England college preparatory school students in my research would make a fascinating comparison. To an extent not approached by even the most ardently moralistic prep schools, such schools do not hesitate to claim that their mixture of religion and academics produces superior moral values and behavior in their students. Indeed, this is often put forth as the primary reason for such schools' existence. Of course, since value systems differ as to just what is and is not "moral behavior," such a study would have to take care to use the schools' own criteria for what constitutes this behavior. Cookson and Persell report that "schools historically associated with trying to exercise social control over their students — Episcopal and Catholic schools — are no more likely to produce perceived change than schools that have allowed students more individuality, such as western and progressive schools" (1985, p. 145). If this is the case — and my results suggest that it is — then the notion of sending one's child to a religious school for a better inculcation of values than at a public school must be seriously questioned.

Possibly one of my study's more important contributions has been the introduction of the technique of obtaining the samples on entry into college, when the students are of legal age and beyond the restraint of school and parents and yet still at a stage where their secondary school experiences are fresh in their minds. The obtaining of both parent and school permission, difficult enough at college prep schools, would almost certainly be impossible at parochial schools. The sampling technique I have used avoids this obstacle.

As I noted in the Introduction, I found a large number of significant differences between my entire study sample, composed of college-bound prep school and public school students, and Sorensen's nationwide probability sample of high school-age adolescents. The fact that these differences largely disappeared when comparisons were made between college-bound prep and public school students suggests that the attitudes and behavior of college-bound adolescents may be considerably different than any random selection of U.S. adolescents, of whom only about one-fourth finish high school and go on to college. If so, perhaps we are living in a "two cultures" society. One is reminded of Benjamin Disraeli's 1845 novel *Sybil*, when a young stranger, in response to the novel's hero Egremont's claim that "our Queen reigns over the greatest nation which ever existed," replies:

> Which nation? For she reigns over two, between which there is no intercourse and no sympathy; they are as ignorant of each other's habits, thoughts and feelings as if they were dwellers in different zones or inhabitants of different planets; who are formed by a different breeding, are fed a different food, and are ordered by different manners and not governed by the same laws.

Here the rift may be the result of the differing quality of education made available to each group. If true, this has profound significance, both in accounting for the existence of wide gaps in American public attitudes and behavior related to certain issues and for emphasizing the need for our education system to be directed toward the narrowing of this gap. In the Spring 1984 issue of *Of Arts and Sciences*, a publication of the University of Virginia College and Graduate School of Arts and Sciences, Michael Marshall, chair of the public school board in Albemarle County, Virginia, notes that:

> Private schools are much more direct about giving information that their students may need to be an elite in society. But because public schools seem to have such low expectations, we get off the mark in the first grades. There is a broadening gap between the knowledge base in public schools and the rising sophistication in private school children. It is a crisis of expectations.

Certainly a high-quality education is one factor, if not *the* factor, pinpointed here — whether access to, aptitude or ambition for, or some other factor, is not clear — as being a major determinant for value-based choices, whether of attitudes or behavior. Note this is not to say that the values and behavior of either group are better or worse; only that they are different. This suggests that voucher proposals, put forth politically under the guise of parental choice, may only serve to widen the gap between students in public and independent schools and do a profound disservice to both.

REFERENCES

Baird, L. *The Elite Schools: A Profile of Prestigious Independent Schools.* Lexington, Mass.: D.C. Heath, 1977.

Belash, Rachel. "Why Girls' Schools Remain Necessary." *New York Times,* 22 February 1988, p. A19.

Birnbach, Lisa, et al. *The Official Preppie Handbook.* New York: Workman, 1980.

Blumenthal, Sidney. "The Cold War and the Closet." *The New Yorker,* 17 March 1997, p. 117.

Bonz, Margaret Huling. "Reflections on Education for Girls and Women: An Independent Project." *Ethel Walker School Alumnae Bulletin* (Fall 1993): 8–9.

Brumberg, Joan Jacob. *The Body Project: An Intimate History of American Girls.* New York: Random House, 1997.

Bullough, Vern L., and Bullough, Bonnie. *Sin, Sickness, and Sanity: A History of Sexual Attitudes.* New York: Garland, 1975.

Caletti, G. "Report of the Sexual Behavior of a Select Group of People." In *Proceeding of the Fifth World Congress of Medical Sexology, Rome 1978, Medical Sexology,* edited by G.R. Forle and W. Pasini. Littleton, Mass.: PSG, 1978.

Compton, William R. "The Great Spiritual Rift." *The News,* Northfield Mount Hermon School (Winter 1988): 14–16.

Cookson, Peter W., and Persell, Caroline Hodges. *Preparing for Power: America's Elite Boarding Schools.* New York: Basic Books, 1985.

Cuneo, Michael W. *The Smoke of Satan.* Baltimore: Johns Hopkins University Press, 1999.

Davies, Nigel. *The Rampant God: Eros Throughout the World.* New York: William Morrow, 1984.

Edmonds, Patricia H. "A Climate of Respect." *Andover Bulletin* (Winter 1995).

Francoeur, R. *Becoming a Sexual Person.* New York: John Wiley and Sons, 1984.

Gathorne-Hardy, Jonathan. *The Old School Tie.* New York: Viking, 1977.

Gilligan, Carol. *In a Different Voice.* Cambridge, Mass.: Harvard University Press, 1982.

Gilligan, Carol, and Brown, Lynn Mikel. *Meeting at the Crossroads: Women's Psychology and Girls' Development.* Cambridge, Mass.: Harvard University Press, 1992.

Goodich, Michael. *The Unmentionable Vice: Homosexuality in the Late Middle Ages*. New Haven, Conn.: Yale University Press, 1977.

Goodwin, Doris Kearns. *The Fitzgeralds and the Kennedys: An American Saga*. New York: Simon and Schuster, 1987.

Graves, Robert. *Goodbye to All That*. London: Jonathan Cape, 1929.

Greenbaum, Vicky. "Bringing Gay and Lesbian Literature Out of the Closet." In *Open Lives, Safe Schools*, edited by Donovan R. Walling. Bloomington, Ind.: Phi Delta Kappa Educational Foundation, 1996.

Haeberle, E. *The Sex Atlas*. New York: Seabury Press, 1978.

Hass, Aaron. *Teenage Sexuality: A Survey of Teenage Sexual Behavior*. New York: Macmillan, 1979.

Hoffman, Joanne. "Looking Beyond Gender." *Concord Academy* (Winter 1994): 2-4.

Justice, B., and Justice, R. *The Broken Taboo: Sex in the Family*. New York: Human Science Press, 1979.

Kantner, J., and Zelnik, M. "Probability of Intercourse and Conception Among U.S. Teenage Women, 1971 and 1976." *Family Planning Perspective* 11 (1979): 177-83.

Kinsey, Alfred C.; Pomeroy, Wardell B.; and Martin, Clyde. *Sexual Behavior of the Human Male*. Philadelphia: W.B. Saunders, 1948.

Kinsey, Alfred C.; Pomeroy, Wardell B.; Martin, Clyde; and Gebhard, Paul H. *Sexual Behavior of the Human Female*. Philadelphia: W.B. Saunders, 1953.

Kirkendall, L. *Premarital Intercourse and Interpersonal Relationships*. New York: Gramercy, 1968.

Lawrence-Lightfoot, Sara. *Respect: An Exploration*. Reading, Mass.: Perseus, 1999.

McLachlan, James. *American Boarding Schools: A Historical Study*. New York: Charles Scribner's Sons, 1970.

Miracle, Andrew W., Jr., and Rees, C. Roger. *Lessons of the Locker Room: The Myth of School Sports*. Buffalo, N.Y.: Prometheus, 1994.

Morgan, Ted. *FDR: A Biography*. New York: Simon and Schuster, 1985.

O'Donnell, Kendra Stearns. *Exeter Bulletin* 22 (Fall 1996).

O'Donnell, Kendra Stearns. "Stepping Back." *Exeter Bulletin* 22 (Summer 1997): 9.

"Of Arts and Sciences." *The College & Graduate School of Arts and Sciences, University of Virginia* 12 (Spring 1994).

Powell, Arthur G. "Melting Down Individualism." *The Independent School* (Spring 1986).

Prescott, J. "Body Pleasures and the Origins of Violence," *The Futurist* 9 (February 1975): 64-75.

Rae, John. *Letters from School.* London: William Collins & Co., 1987.

Sacred Congregation for the Doctrine of the Faith. *Declaration on Sexual Ethics.* Washington, D.C.: U.S. Conference of Catholic Bishops, 29 December 1975.

Schefler, W. *Statistics for the Biological Sciences.* Reading, Mass.: Addison-Wesley, 1979.

Sedgwick, John. "World Without End." *New England Monthly* 5 (September 1988): 53-57, 109.

Sizer, Theodore. *Horace's Compromise: The Dilemma of the American High School.* Boston: Houghton-Mifflin, 1984.

Sorensen, Robert C. *Adolescent Sexuality in Contemporary America.* New York: Times Mirror, 1973.

Sours, K. *An Introduction to the SCSS Conversational System.* New York: McGraw-Hill, 1982.

Sprole, Frank. *Hotchkiss Magazine* (Fall 1998).

"Three Questions: Three Headmasters." *Bulletin of Miss Porter's School* (Spring 1987): 2-5.

Turner, Meg, and Vorkink, Christiaan. "Students Reap Coeducation's Rewards." *Exeter Bulletin* (Fall 1995): 7.

Valentini, N., and di Meglio, C. *Sex and the Confessional.* New York: Stein & Day, 1975.

Vener, A., and Stewart, C. "Adolescent Sexual Behavior in Middle America Revisited, 1970-1973." *Journal of Marriage and the Family* 36 (1974): 728-35.

Vorkink, Peter, II. "When East Meets West." *Bulletin of Phillips Exeter Academy* 88 (Summer 1993): 7-8.

Wilcox, Tom. "Teaching in the Nineties." *Concord Academy* (Spring/Summer 1995): 6.

Wilson, E.O. *Sociobiology: The New Synthesis.* Cambridge, Mass.: Belknap Press of Harvard University Press, 1975.

ABOUT THE AUTHOR

Barbara Bernache-Baker's teaching career in New England college preparatory schools spans more than 30 years, beginning in 1952 at Cushing Academy in Ashburnham, Massachusetts, and ending in 1986 at the Loomis Chaffee School in Windsor, Connecticut. From 1955 to 1962 she taught biology at the Northfield School for Girls and Mount Hermon School for Boys (now the coeducational Northfield Mount Hermon) in Massachusetts. Called "the consummate prep school teacher" by one of the six headmasters under whom she has worked, Bernache-Baker's many awards include a Science Department Chair at Loomis Chaffee, a YWCA Woman of the Year award for outstanding contributions in education, and being named a Danforth Foundation Associate.

With her biologist husband, Bernache-Baker has taught a course in human sexuality at Wesleyan University in Middletown, Connecticut. She has presented papers at three World Congresses (Rome, 1978; Washington, D. C., 1983; and New Delhi, 1985) on the topics of sexuality and religion, sexuality and feminism, and adolescent sexuality, respectively.

Working in her specialty as a marine biologist, Bernache-Baker is currently director of the Vieques Conservation and Historical Trust on the island of Vieques, Puerto Rico, where she has resided for the past several years. She also is the author of two conservation-directed booklets, *The Bioluminescent Bays of Vieques* and *The Mangrove Forests of Vieques*.